DATE DUE

APR 1 7 2006	12/13/11
MAY 1 5 2006	
APR 2 8 2007	

DEMCO, INC. 38-2931

William Blake

Updated Edition

Twayne's English Authors Series

Herb Sussman, Editor

Northeastern University

TEAS 202

PORTRAIT OF WILLIAM BLAKE BY THOMAS PHILLIPS.
By courtesy of the National Portrait Gallery, London.

William Blake

Updated Edition

Victor N. Paananen

Michigan State University

Twayne Publishers
An Imprint of Simon & Schuster Macmillan
New York

Prentice Hall International
London Mexico City New Delhi Singapore Sydney Toronto

Twayne's English Authors Series No. 202

William Blake: Updated Edition
Victor N. Paananen

Twayne Publishers
An Imprint of Simon & Schuster Macmillan
1633 Broadway
New York, NY 10019

Library of Congress Cataloging-in-Publication Data
Paananen, Victor N.
   William Blake updated edition / Victor N. Paananen
      p. cm. — (Twayne's English authors series ; TEAS 202)
   Includes bibliographical references and index.
   ISBN 0-8057-7053-4
   1. Blake, William, 1757–1827—Criticism and interpretation. I. Title. II. Series.
PR4147.P25 1996
821'.7—dc20   95-25616
                                                                                      CIP

The paper used in this publication meets the minimum requirements of American
National Standard for Information Sciences—Permanence of Paper for Printed Library
Materials, ANSI Z39.48-1984. ∞™

10 9 8 7 6 5 4 3 2 1

Printed in the United States of America

In Memory of My Father
Niles Henry Paananen
(1910–1956)

Contents

Preface to William Blake: Updated Edition

When I published my *William Blake* in the Twayne English Authors Series in 1977, a substantial library of Blake criticism and commentary already existed. Since then, however, the floodgates have opened, and books on Blake have appeared at what has seemed an ever accelerating rate. Indeed between 1972, when I finished the first draft of *William Blake,* and 1977, when it was copyedited and already in a need of some updating—which I tried hastily to provide—the new outpouring of Blake books had begun. I had predicted in my 1977 "Conclusion" that the "wildfire spread of interest in Blake's work among students" would help to shape opposition to the social and intellectual foundations of our civilization; throughout the 1970s, 1980s, and 1990s, however, this interest has produced instead more books on Blake. I also predicted that "Blake's theology [would] receive serious attention in the future." Although serious critics no longer deny Blake's Christian stance, the best writing about Blake's ideas has come from young scholars interested not in Blake's Christianity as much as the similarity between Blake and Marx: the common ground between Blake's refusal to be enslaved by the categories of formal logic and the dialectical thought of Hegel and Marx; the way Blake's reconciliation of subject and object in experience antici- pates Marx; and whether Blake's objections to the "mind-forg'd mana- cles" of his culture are not an early version of the Marxist insight into ideology and the hegemonic. Blake studies have taken a Marxist turn.

In many cases, a Marxist reading of Blake has been qualified with an assurance that the critic does not mean to see Blake as a "proto-Marx"[1] or "a premature practitioner of Marxist dialectic"[2]; but some outstanding Marxist writing on Blake has not hesitated to show that Blake and Marx began from premises that were often similar and then thought their way through to conclusions that were virtually the same. Minna Doskow's brilliant essay "The Humanized Universe of Blake and Marx" (1982) seems to me to be the single most useful direct comparison of Blake and Marx, because it operates at the most fundamental philosophic level. The paper explains how each reached a similar solution to the impasse in bourgeois philosophy on the issue of "the relation of human subjectivity to the external world."[3]

In *Blake, Hegel, and Dialectic* (1982), David Punter convincingly and usefully placed Blake within the history of dialectic thought that would culminate in Marx. In her far-ranging *War of the Titans* (1983), Jackie DiSalvo pointed to ideas shared by Blake and Marx in many areas and demonstrated that in *The Four Zoas* Blake's reading of human history is the one that Marx would later offer. A Marxist understanding of Blake also infuses Michael Ferber's excellent *The Social Vision of William Blake* (1985); other important Marxist readings of Blake have come from, among others, John Brenkman, Stewart Crehan, Heather Glen, and Edward Larrissy.

My original *William Blake* emphasized Blake's visionary Christianity and suggested that its sources need not be in Dissent, as is usually asserted, but can be found within the emerging Evangelical movement in the Church of England.[4] Such an emphasis gives a special significance within Blake's mythic system to the fall and restoration of "Lambeth," the seat of the Anglican Church, and causes one to see an appeal for changed doctrines *within* the Church as a theme of a work such as *Jerusalem.* Although I did my best to tie Blake's concerns to the religious issues of the age, I did not sufficiently emphasize that many of his ideas also participated in a long tradition of antinomianism and radical politics stretching backward to the English Revolution and beyond. It was A. L. Morton who first demonstrated that Blake's assertion of the divinity present in each individual, and his denunciation of the Moral Law as irrelevant to a religion based on the forgiveness of sins, had previously been voiced by a group in the English Civil War known as the Ranters. Désirée Hirst, in her *Hidden Riches* (1964), traced the origins of some of these ideas far back in time. In the Evangelical movement of the eighteenth and nineteenth centuries, especially through the influence of William Law within that movement, these earlier voices of vision and revolt were again heard.

When I began to think about an approach to an updated version of *William Blake* in 1993, an especially important work on Blake appeared that shared my interest in the religious climate of Blake's England. This book, *Witness against the Beast: William Blake and the Moral Law* by E. P. Thompson, examined doctrines of a group influenced by the Ranters that actually survived into Blake's time and beyond. The group that Thompson studied was the Muggletonians, a sect to which Blake's mother possibly belonged. Added to the book's concern with both contemporary and long-term religious currents was an appreciation of William Blake written from the point of view of one of the world's most respected Marxists. Thompson saw that Blake's sincere Christianity was expressed in a language that also embodied the opposition of ordinary British people to the ruling powers of the age: "it struck very precisely at critical positions of the hegemonic culture, the 'common sense' of the ruling groups" (Thompson, 110). Thompson did not succeed in proving that the Muggletonians were the group most influential on Blake, and he did not make use of either Minna Doskow's analysis of Blake's philosophic foundations or David Punter's search for the roots of Blake's dialectical thought to place Blake and Marx within the same tradition. But this distinguished scholar, through a book finished just before his death, confirmed my belief that a Christian-Marxist dialogue was now a feature of Blake studies that needed to be represented in an updating of my original *William Blake* (and Blake seems to offer his encouragement for such an approach by asking, "Are not Religion & Politics the Same Thing?"[5]). Thompson was amused to call himself a "Muggletonian Marxist"; *William Blake: Updated Edition* endeavors to see more of the Marxist in the Muggletonian—or at any rate in the Christian—Blake than the first version of this book did. John Brenkman has written that a "juxtaposition of Blake and Marx" is useful not so much "to place Blake within Marx's frame of reference but to resituate Marx within a *political* and *cultural* process that includes, as a productive and prophetic moment, the poetry of Blake."[6] The common features of the dialectical thought of Marx and Blake make it no anachronism to speak of Blake in the Marxist language of "alienation" and "division of labor." Blake's "contraries" and "abstraction" might similarly provide a vocabulary for discussing Karl Marx, but he is not the subject of this book.

The common roots of Marxism and Romanticism are at times neglected, but, as Ernst Fischer pointed out, Marx emerged from the "romantic revolt against a world which turned everything into a commodity and degraded man to the status of an object. . . . [The] poets and philosophers . . . complained that man had become a fragment of his own self, had been overpowered by his own works, had fallen from himself."[7] Blake and Marx each chose dialectical thought over formal logic, stressed activity over contemplation, and called on us to intervene in the material world itself to begin to transform it into a fully human world. In words that John Brenkman applies to Marx, both saw "culture as a set of material-social practices" (Brenkman, 231). In the pages that follow, I extend my earlier reading of Blake to capture more of the side of Blake that anticipates Marx. If this approach captures a more political Blake, or one with extensive social insight, it will perhaps support the

predictions for his influence on our culture in my original conclusion—
and will also second E. P. Thompson's assertion that Blake's work is, like
Marx's, "a plank in the floor upon which the future must walk"
(Thompson, 228).

Despite my concern with explaining aspects of Blake within both
Christian and Marxist thought, I do not feel that a book in this series
should primarily argue a thesis. As with the first version, my first task is
to guide the reader entering the sometimes bewildering maze of myth,
radical politics, and visionary Christianity that Blake creates in his major
works and implies in his lesser work. *William Blake* (1977) has, I hope,
proved to be a useful tool that will continue to help the reader concerned
primarily with Blake's Christian outlook. The preface to that book follows because I think that it is important to restate its relationship to a
tradition of Blake scholarship to which every reader of Blake owes a debt
of gratitude; but I would like also to offer this reminder that within
William Blake: Updated Edition remains the structure and most of the
content of the earlier work.

Preface to William Blake *(1977)*

This book, a brief, introductory account of the writings of William Blake, appears at a time when Blake studies are characterized by increased and healthy specialization. At last, now that Blake has escaped the status of a cult figure, scholars are able to work systematically at the details of his myth and the particulars of his sources. The critical work of S. Foster Damon, Northrop Frye, David Erdman, Harold Bloom, and several others has given us a Blake that we recognize as a major poet and whom we begin to understand. The textual, bibliographical, and biographical work of Geoffrey Keynes, David Erdman, G. E. Bentley, Jr., and others has provided trustworthy apparatus for scholarship and has shed a little light on an obscure life. Specialized work can now be carried forward confidently; at the same time, a book like this one can be written with fewer trepidations. Blake scholars will no doubt dispute many of my readings of individual poems and passages—many of the readings are indeed new—but they will recognize that I am writing about the same William Blake that the scholarship of the last 50 years has identified for us.

My brief account of Blake's life, heavily indebted to the excellent *Blake Records* of G. E. Bentley, Jr., is put forward to provide as accurate a context for Blake's work as possible while sticking to the sparse facts. The remainder of the book is an account of Blake's opinions on life, eternity, art, and vision that is carried out by means of a survey of his writings that is usually chronological. But a significant exception to this type of organization is *The Book of Urizen,* which is discussed somewhat earlier in the book than its date would justify, because its brief treatment of Blake's major themes gives it special value as an introduction to Blake's thought and art. Because of Blake's reputation for obscurity, I make extensive use of quotation both to explicate the lines and to demonstrate that Blake can speak very well for himself. The William Blake who emerges from this study is an opponent of rational theology but an advocate of visionary Christianity; he is an uncompromising supporter of freedom from all institutions, laws, and moral codes; he is a Christian anarchist who is highly successful in finding myth and method, both to communicate his objections to our psychological bondage and to show us the perfect liberty to which unchained Imagination and Energy can lead us.

Acknowledgments

I wish to thank the Michigan State University Library, the London Library, and the British Library for providing needed books and pleasant working conditions for my work on this book. I would also like to thank the College of Arts and Letters of Michigan State University for the assignment to research during which I completed it. My debts to my wife, Donna, are too many to name, but I profited greatly from her advice about word processing—as I did also from our son Karl's wizardry in providing me with a computer-scanned version of my 1977 *William Blake* to work with. I am grateful to the editor of this series, Professor Herbert Sussman of Northeastern University, for his excellent suggestions for strengthening the book, and to Anne Davidson and India Koopman of Twayne Publishers for seeing me through copyediting and production.

I am also grateful to the National Portrait Gallery in London for permission to reproduce the portrait of William Blake by Thomas Phillips as the frontispiece to this book; to the Pierpont Morgan Library in New York for permission to reproduce the title page of *The Book of Urizen*; and to Harvard University for permission to reproduce both "The Sick Rose" from the Harvard copy of *Songs of Innocence and of Experience* and Plates 32 and 57 from the Harvard copy of *Jerusalem*.

Acknowledgments (1977)

I wish to thank Michigan State University for assignment to research duties in the summer of 1972, and for an All-University Research Grant that has helped with expenses in the production of a typescript. The Michigan State University Library and the London Library, St. James's Square, have generously provided books and a place to work on projects related to the subject of this book.

I have already suggested the indebtedness of this book to previous Blake scholarship. I wish to acknowledge further the general indebtedness of any critical work that I undertake to Professor Karl Kroeber, now at Columbia University, but whose courses at the University of Wisconsin were not only brilliant expositions of the literature and civilization of nineteenth-century England but also stimulating demonstrations of new possibilities for the criticism of imaginative literature. To my wife Donna I owe my mental and corporeal survival in the years that we have devoted to the academic life.

Chronology

1757   William Blake born 28 November at 28 Broad Street, London, son of James Blake, a shopkeeper. Baptized 11 December in St. James's Church, Piccadilly.

c. 1765–1767   Sees "a tree filled with angels" on Peckham Rye.

1772–1779   Apprenticed to James Basire, engraver. Probably lives with Basire's family at 31 Great Queen Street, Lincoln's Inn Fields. In 1774, begins sketching memorials in Westminster Abbey for Basire.

1779   Admitted as a student to the Royal Academy of Arts in October.

1780   Unwillingly caught in a mob storming Newgate Prison 6 June during anti-Catholic riots. With James Parker, another former apprentice of James Basire, and Thomas Stothard, a young artist, taken prisoner in October by British soldiers who mistake the three young men making sketches along the River Medway for French spies.

1782   Marries Catherine Boucher 18 August in St. Mary's Church, Battersea.

1783   Printing of *Poetical Sketches* arranged by John Flaxman and the Reverend and Mrs. Anthony Stephen Mathew.

1784   After his father's death in July, opens a printshop in partnership with James Parker. The Blakes reside in Soho, first in Broad Street, then in Poland Street, until 1790.

1787   Death of his brother Robert, aged 19. Sees Robert's spirit rise to heaven, "clapping its hands for joy." Subsequently, Robert reveals method of illuminated printing to him in a dream.

1788   Publishes *There Is No Natural Religion* and *All Religions Are One.*

1789   On 13 April signs list of 32 resolutions passed at a founding convention of a New Church based on the teachings of Emanuel Swedenborg. Engraves and publishes *Songs of Innocence* and *Book of Thel*. About this time writes, but does not engrave or publish, *Tiriel*.

1790   Writes *The Marriage of Heaven and Hell*. Moves to 13 Hercules Buildings in Lambeth, where the Blakes will live for 10 years.

1791   Prepares *The French Revolution* for the press, but it is not printed. Does engravings for John Gabriel Stedman's *Narrative of a Five Years' Expedition against the Revolted Negroes of Surinam* (not published until 1796).

1793   Prospectus offers *America, Visions of the Daughters of Albion, Thel, The Marriage of Heaven and Hell, Songs of Innocence, Songs of Experience*.

1794   Publishes *Songs of Innocence and of Experience, Europe, Book of Urizen*.

1795   Publishes *Book of Ahania, Book of Los,* and *Song of Los*.

1796   Illustrates Edward Young's *Night Thoughts*.

1797   At work on *Vala* (subsequently *The Four Zoas*).

1800   Takes cottage at Felpham in Sussex made available by William Hayley.

1803   Forced to evict a soldier named Scolfield from his garden at Felpham. Scolfield brings charges of sedition. Returns to London to 17 South Moulton Street.

1804   Tried and acquitted at Chichester. Starts *Milton* (published 1809–10) and *Jerusalem* (published 1818–20). Visits Truchsessian Gallery.

1808   Edition of Robert Blair's *Grave*, illustrated by Blake, published.

1809   Exhibits paintings at 28 Broad Street and writes *Descriptive Catalogue*. Exhibition attacked by Robert Hunt in the *Examiner* as "fresh proof of the alarming increase of the effects of insanity."

1815–1818   Engraves for Wedgwood catalogues. In 1816 illustrates John Milton's "L'Allegro" and "Il Penseroso."

1821   Moves to modest rooms in Fountain Court, Strand.

1824   Illustrates John Bunyan's *Pilgrim's Progress*.

1826   Publishes his illustrations to the Book of Job.

1827   At work on illustrations of Dante's *Divine Comedy* until his death on 12 August. Buried in Bunhill Fields Burying Ground, the Dissenters' cemetery, but with the rites of the Church of England.

57

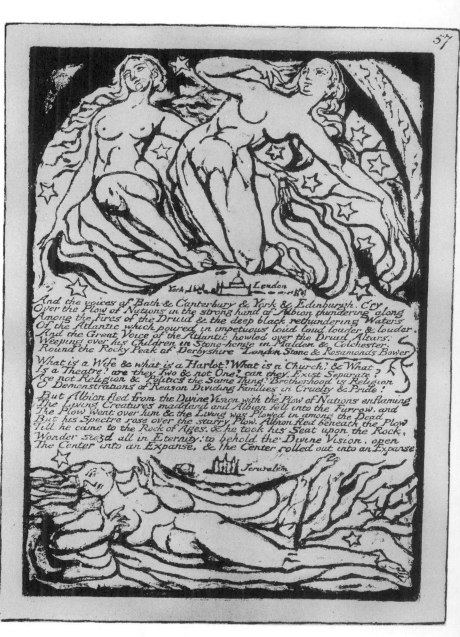

And the voices of Bath & Canterbury & York & Edinburgh. Cry
Over the Plow of Nations in the strong hand of Albion thundering along
Among the fires of the Druid & the deep black rethundering Waters
Of the Atlantic which poured in impetuous loud loud. louder & louder.
And the Great Voice of the Atlantic howled over the Druid Altars:
Weeping over his Children in Stone-henge in Malden & Colchester.
Round the Rocky Peak of Derbyshire London Stone & Rosamonds Bower

What is a Wife & what is a Harlot? What is a Church? & What
Is a Theatre? are they Two & not One? can they Exist Separate?
Are not Religion & Politics the Same Thing? Brotherhood is Religion
O Demonstrations of Reason Dividing Families in Cruelty & Pride!

But Albion fled from the Divine Vision, with the Plow of Nations enflaming
The Living Creatures maddend and Albion fell into the Furrow. and
The Plow went over him & the Living was Plowed in among the Dead.
But his Spectre rose over the starry Plow. Albion fled beneath the Plow
Till he came to the Rock of Ages. & he took his Seat upon the Rock.
Wonder seizd all in Eternity! to behold the Divine Vision. open
The Center into an Expanse, & the Center rolled out into an Expanse

Chapter One

Life and Times

Because very little is known about the life of William Blake, conjecture has often supplied the place of fact in the writing of his biography. The few authentic accounts that we have of Blake picture a life of hard work and frequent disappointment, indeed of poverty and obscurity, that he faced with stout courage and unfailing cheerfulness.[1] So little in the records satisfies any sentimental notion of what we would have our inspired—or mad—poet be that we conclude that the real truths are yet to be found. Conversely, the intellectual movements that touched Blake in eighteenth-century London, and perhaps found their synthesis in him, seem to be too many and too confusedly entwined to satisfy our scrutiny any more than the biographical details do. We know that Blake's friends were Deists and Swedenborgians, Unitarians and Anglicans—but Blake himself can be found to be critical of aspects of each of these positions, at least from time to time.

If we seek less evident components in Blake's intellectual milieu—the Neoplatonism of Thomas Taylor, the mysticism of Jacob Boehme, or the alchemical philosophy of Paracelsus—we have to admit to a quite disappointing degree of correspondence between what Blake has to say and what any one of these thinkers had said. No one influence of the several possible influences on Blake serves to explain Blake's thought—not that the thought of an independent and creative thinker can ever be so explained—but, taken together, they form the rich context out of which Blake's work took shape. This philosophic context serves, in fact, as the source of all British Romantic thought; for William Wordsworth, Samuel Taylor Coleridge, and even Percy Shelley emerge from the same intellectual milieu, despite the wide divergences in outlook that exist among them and between each of them and Blake. Like the other British Romantic poets, Blake found himself in an era characterized by new attitudes and approaches in philosophy, theology, and politics.

The Evangelical Movement

The complex synthesis that formed the Romantic intellectual climate is much the same as the synthesis of influences that had taken place in theology during the eighteenth century in what is called "the Evangelical Movement." Probably William Law (1686–1761), the author of *Christian Perfection* and *A Serious Call* who had himself been a disciple of Jacob Boehme, had been the greatest influence on Christians who would later be Evangelicals—or Methodists[2] or even Swedenborgians.[3] Law had helped to inculcate a new respect for emotion and "mysticism" in religion, and he had laid the basis for the attack on rational Deism that the Evangelical clergy would lead. Blake makes no secret of his admiration for Evangelicals such as John Wesley and George Whitefield; and he defends "Methodists," members of the new sect formed by a group of Evangelicals driven from the Church of England. Indeed, there seems to be considerable merit in T. B. Shepherd's relatively casual observation that "the greatest poet of the Evangelical Revival was William Blake."[4] If nothing else, the background provided by an awareness of the progress of the Evangelical movement helps us recognize that many of Blake's ideas had analogues and "context" within his own age.

At the heart of the Evangelical Revival, as of Romanticism, was a rejection of the impersonal and in fact threatening natural world that Newtonian physics had produced. So-called Natural Theology tried to construct arguments for Christianity that were based on observation of such a universe. Where such theology seemed inevitably to lead, however, was to Deism, which concludes that God has created the perfection of Nature and then departed from the world. The Evangelicals recognized that such reasoning about a natural world separate from humanity was based on a false division between perceiving subject and perceived object: in human experience and in human activity, subject and object are one. This recognition restored a meaningful universe, one created in fact through human emotion and the activity of the human imagination.

In Evangelical theology, emotion and vision—both instances of how the human mind creates the kind of world that humans occupy—were encouraged and not suppressed in favor of a divisive rationality. Fervent preaching and the singing of highly emotional hymns—the Evangelicals were the most prolific hymn writers in the history of English Christianity—came increasingly to characterize religious worship. Although the emotions that were so important to Christian belief were felt by individuals, they were also universal, common to all humanity: indeed they were God shared by all humanity, as the traditional Christian formula, "He in us, and we in Him," had always said. Such an outlook leads quickly to the social correlative that all are equal and to the moral position that an innate divinity need not concern itself with externally imposed rules of conduct.

Arguments of this sort had been heard in the English Revolution in the seventeenth century and still survived in tiny sects such as the Muggletonians. They were implicit, however, in the Evangelical solution of what Minna Doskow has called "the central philosophical problem" of what would be the nineteenth century of both Blake and Marx, "the relation of human subjectivity to the external world" (Doskow 1982a, 225). Some Evangelicals left or were asked to leave the Church of England, becoming thereby part of organized Dissent, but Anglican Evangelicals grew in numbers and influence and soon occupied influential pulpits and positions in Church leadership.

When William Blake was born on 28 November 1757 in a house on the no-longer-fashionable Broad Street (now Broadwick Street) in Soho, the Evangelical movement in the Church of England was already moving toward the important position it would attain in the nineteenth century. "Every Christian under their scheme," Prime Minister William Gladstone wrote of the Evangelicals, "had personal dealings with his God and Saviour. The inner life was again acknowledged as a reality, and substituted for that bare, bald compromise between the seen and the unseen world which reduces the share of the 'far more exceeding and eternal' almost to *nil.*"[5] Evangelical impulses seem to have reached Blake through Anglican rather than Dissenting sources. Blake was baptized into the Church of England at St. James's Church, Piccadilly, on 11 December, two weeks after his birth. Blake's father may later have joined a Dissenting group,[6] but Blake's Anglican baptism, marriage, and burial all suggest that Blake's allegiances were to the Church of England and not to Dissent.[7] The Blakes were very much a part of the life of the Parish of St. James, where William's father, James, supplied some haberdashery needs of the charity school (*BRS,* 2–8).[8] (Blake would express his regret at the passing of the Dean of Canterbury in 1825, remembering him in his former role as Rector of St. James.[9]) Still, whatever the source of Blake's introduction to visionary religion, we do know that between the ages of 8 and 10 he had rejected the "compromise between the seen and the unseen" with which most Christians of the preceding age had been contented:

> On Peckham Rye (by Dulwich Hill) it is, as he will in after years relate, that while quite a child, of eight or ten perhaps, he had his "first vision." Sauntering along, the boy looks up and sees a tree filled with angels,

bright angelic wings bespangling every bough like stars. Returned home
he relates the incident, and only through his mother's intercession escapes
a thrashing from his honest father, for telling a lie. Another time, one
summer morn, he sees the haymakers at work, and amid them angelic
figures walking. (Gilchrist, 1, 7)

To see "angels" in this fashion is, in Gladstone's phrase, to acknowledge
"the Inner Life" as "a reality."[10] Blake was to argue forcefully in *There Is
No Natural Religion* and elsewhere for the superiority of this mode of perception over the "compromise" of what he terms "ratio" vision.

Blake's boyhood circumstances were humble but not poverty-strick-
en, thanks to his father's prospering shop. Blake's politics were generally
those of his class in London—that of shopkeepers and artisans—and
thus Blake was always a "Liberty Boy." He would join Dissenters and
Deists in supporting the French Revolution when it came; and he did so
not only for reasons of class and religious conviction but because he
clearly saw how poverty, vice, and civic brutality were perpetuated by
both church and state. Indeed, as Stanley Gardner has effectively
demonstrated, every social evil of the age was fully visible within yards
of Blake's boyhood home.[11] He would attack many of the institutionally
supported horrors of the era in some of the most destructively analytic
poems in his *Songs of Experience*. But, in the meantime, he had to meet
the obligations of his class; and, having first attended a drawing school,
he was apprenticed to James Basire, an engraver.

From Basire, Blake learned the trade that sustained him, perhaps
not very well at times, for the rest of his life. Assigned to sketch the
monuments in Westminster Abbey, Blake developed rapidly as an
artist. But the isolation and the silence of the Abbey freed him to
attend to the reality of his inner life again: "It was when he was one
day thus secluded in the dim vaulted solitude of Westminster Abbey
that he saw, as he afterwards records, one of his visions. The aisles and
galleries of the old building (or sanctuary) suddenly filled with a great
procession of monks and priests, choristers and censer-bearers, and his
entranced ear heard the chant of plain-song and chorale, while the
vaulted roof trembled to the sound of music."[12] The source of Blake's
art was never to be the external world or the models provided by the
work of others; instead, his source was always to be his own vision;
and, in the incident in the Abbey, it allowed him to see the living
meaning of the structure rather than the dead stone that he had been
assigned to sketch.

Opponents and Allies

By October 1779, when Blake was admitted as a student to the Royal Academy of Art, it was already too late for him to accept the artistic practice or habits of mind of the preceding age. Blake's encounter with Sir Joshua Reynolds, the president of the academy and a great painter of the late eighteenth century, demonstrates this fundamental aversion to Neoclassical caution and precision: "'Once I remember his talking to me of Reynolds,' writes a surviving friend: 'he became furious at what the latter had dared to say of his early works. When a very young man he had called on Reynolds to show him some designs, and had been recommended to work with less extravagance and more simplicity, and to correct his drawing. This Blake seemed to regard as an affront never to be forgotten'" (Gilchrist 1, 267).

Reynolds's recommendations for the checking of enthusiasm and for the submission to compromises helped to make Reynolds serve as Blake's model for the very enemy of Inspiration: "Reynolds's Opinion was that Genius May be Taught & that all Pretence to Inspiration is a Lie & a Deceit, to say the least of it. For if it is a Deceit, the whole Bible is Madness" (*CW,* 452). Or, more directly, Blake's view of Reynolds was that "This Man was Hired to Depress Art" (*CW,* 445). Blake's inability to work to the standards of a Reynolds was to be one major reason for his lack of a public as an artist—and as a poet—for the rest of his life.

In Blake's responses to Reynolds over the years—primarily expressed in marginal comments to Reynolds's writings—there are hints of another sort of feeling engendered by Blake's contact with the Royal Academy and the "official" artists. Blake sees Reynolds as willing to "Serve Nobility & Fashionable Taste"; and he argues that "Albert Dürer," an artist Blake admired deeply, "would never have got his Manners from the Nobility" (*CW,* 940). E. P. Thompson feels that Blake had absorbed from the "pockets of radical Dissent among the trades . . . a stubborn lack of deference, both social and intellectual" (Thompson, 112), but there is no evidence of Blake's participation in any specifically political activity in these years other than his being caught up by a mob storming Newgate Prison during the Gordon riots directed against the Roman Catholics in 1780:

> On . . . Tuesday, 6th of June, "the Mass-houses" having already been demolished—one, in Blake's near neighborhood, Warwick Street, Golden Square—and various private houses also; the rioters, flushed with

gin and victory, were turning their attention to grander schemes of dev-
astation. That evening, the artist happened to be walking in a route chosen by one of the mobs at large, whose course lay from Justice Hyde's
house near Leicester Fields, for the destruction of which less than an hour
had sufficed, through Long Acre, past the quiet house of Blake's old master, engraver Basire, in Great Queen Street, Lincoln's Inn Fields, and
down Holborn, bound for Newgate. Suddenly, he encountered the
advancing wave of triumphant Blackguardism, and was forced (for from
such a great surging mob there is no disentanglement) to go along in the
very front rank, and witness the storm and burning of the fortress-like
prison, and release of its three hundred inmates. (Gilchrist, 1, 35)

Blake's involvement in this night of destruction was involuntary—if
anything he admired the Roman Catholic Church[13]—but the Gordon
riots involved, as James King points out, "members of Blake's own arti-
san class, fearful of losing their jobs to Irish blacklegers." Indeed, Lord
George Gordon himself "was suspicious that the government's toleration
of Papists was based on a desire to pave the way for sending Catholic soldiers to fight against the Americans."[14] The reprehensible violence arose
both from the struggle for work in a rapidly evolving commercial society
and from a desire to protect the gains of a revolution that Blake himself
supported.

In the same year, Blake along with fellow artist Thomas Stothard and
Blake's fellow former apprentice with Basire, James Parker, were arrest-
ed by British soldiers while sketching along the River Medway. Members
of the Royal Academy had to testify in their behalf before the military
were persuaded that the young artists were not French spies. The
American Revolution had revealed British power to be precarious, and
events like the Gordon riots seemed to presage conflagration within
Britain itself. Blake would always celebrate the forces of change; but this
brief period of detention revealed that he lived in a nation-state fully
alert to threats to its continuance in its existing form.

Blake, writes E. P. Thompson, "had been taught in childhood to place
a critical distance between himself and the Rich and Great" (Thompson,
111), and his marriage in 1782 would not have received much attention
in the world of "Fashionable Taste" that Blake had rejected when he
refused to accept Reynolds's guidance. After an unsuccessful courtship of
"a lively little girl" named Polly Wood, who was herself "in a humbler
class" (BR, 21), Blake met Catherine Sophia Boucher, who, we are told,
pitied him because of his recent amatory disappointment and thus won
his heart. Catherine, the daughter of a market gardener in Battersea,

signed the marriage register with an "X," presumably because she was illiterate. Catherine's circumstances, "respectable and industrious" but by no means fashionable, are, therefore, yet another reminder that Blake's world was not that of the Royal Academy and official art (even though he would continue to have a few contacts with the academy, some of them valuable). Catherine was the thirteenth child of the Bouchers, who continued to grow poorer as the years went by.

To those who knew them, William and Catherine seemed well suited. William Gilchrist's well-known tribute to Catherine, based on the testimony of people in the Blake circle, is somewhat patronizing in tone but depicts a sensitive, courageous, and able woman:

> Catherine . . . was endowed with a loving loyal nature, an adaptive open mind, capable of profiting by good teaching, and of enabling her, under constant high influence, to become a meet companion to her imaginative husband in his solitary and wayward course. Uncomplainingly and helpfully, she shared the low and rugged fortunes which overoriginality ensured as his unvarying lot in life. She had mind and the ambition which follows. Not only did she prove a good housewife on straitened means, but in afteryears, under his tuition and hourly companionship, she acquired, besides the useful arts of reading and writing, that which very few uneducated women with the honestest effort ever succeeded in attaining: some footing of equality with her husband. She in time came to work off his engravings as though she had been bred to the trade; nay, imbibed enough of his very own spirit to reflect it in Design which might almost have been his own." (Gilchrist, 1, 38)

Although it has been usual to sum up the young Catherine Boucher as the "illiterate daughter of a Battersea market-gardener,"[15] if one recalls the suffering for both parties that characterized the marriages of S. T. Coleridge and Lord Byron and the first marriage (and to a large extent the second) of Percy Shelley, it is evident that Catherine and William had in their marriage the advantages of a shared talent and similarities in outlook and temperament. When their circumstances for a time permitted the Blakes to consider hiring a servant, Catherine, who had herself been a domestic servant, felt awkward in the role of employer; and William instead performed as many household tasks as his engraving work at home allowed. There were some tensions early in the marriage; but, 17 years on, a close acquaintance could report them to be "as fond of each other, as if their Honey Moon were still shining" (*BR*, 106).

Although Blake's central concern through his period of apprentice-
ship and during his time at the Royal Academy would necessarily be his
drawing, painting, and engraving, he did produce some poetry during
his adolescence and young manhood. Many of the efforts were songs,
sometimes fairly conventional but often charming, that Blake is known
to have sung to music of his own composition. As Martin K. Nurmi has
shown, much of the metrical innovation that readers see in these early
songs and in Blake's later lyrics is in fact the result of Blake's first writing verse with music in mind. Blake, Nurmi explains, "had no interest in
regular metres unless they served the musical effects he wanted, and he
had the confidence to trust his own ear as to what these should be."
Often, "musical and verbal rhythms pull against each other . . . to create
a rhythmical tension."[16] In addition to writing songs, Blake offered his
responses to the poetic fashions of the age in ballad imitations ("Gwin,
King of Norway" and "Fair Elenor"), in a fragment of pseudo-
Elizabethan play ("King Edward the Third"), and in Ossianic prose
poems.

Today, many of these productions remain of considerable interest
because of their hints of the ideas and the methods that the mature
Blake employed. In them we see Blake moving toward the creation of
his later mythic figures in personifications of the seasons (influenced by
James Thomson) and in biblical and historical characters made to carry
symbolic weight. To Samuel C. Chew, the Gothic verse narrative "Fair
Elenor" reveals "an impassioned intensity beyond the capabilities of any
Gothicizer,"[17] and Chew's remark reminds us that each of Blake's imitative works in eighteenth-century modes possesses his characteristic energy. Indeed, these experiments, when considered with the songs, stand as
proof that Blake, although he eventually became a major Romantic poet,
might well rank as the greatest of "pre-Romantic" poets. For the preservation of these works we are indebted to Blake's friends: the Reverend
A. S. Mathew, the clergyman of Percy Chapel (a situation subsequently
filled by important Anglican Evangelicals[18]), who was also the afternoon
preacher at St. Martin's-in-the-Fields; Harriet Mathew, his wife; and
John Flaxman, the sculptor, who arranged the printing of these pieces as
Poetical Sketches (1783) "By W. B."

Although the exact constitution of these social gatherings remains
unknown, Blake seems to have met with friends such as the Mathews
and Flaxman for evenings like the one recorded in the unpublished
satiric piece *An Island in the Moon* (which Blake must have written about
1784–85, perhaps to be read at an occasion such as he describes in it).

Whoever the models for the characters were, this rough burlesque is notable for its satire on the type of unimaginative inquirer that Blake later called "the Idiot Questioner" by characters called "the Antiquarian" and "Obtuse Angle" (the latter often identified as Mathew, but quite possibly the Platonist Thomas Taylor, with whom Blake studied geometry):

> "Reason, Sir?" said the Antiquarian. "I'll give you an example for your reason. As I was walking along the street I saw a vast number of swallows on the rails of an old Gothic square. They seem'd to be going on their passage, as Pliny says. As I was looking up, a little outré fellow, pulling me by the sleeve, cries, 'Pray, Sir, who do all they belong to?' I turn'd myself about with great contempt. Said I, 'Go along, you fool!' 'Fool!' said he, 'who do you call fool? I only ask'd you a civil question.' I had a great mind to have thrash'd the fellow, only he was bigger than I." (*CW*, 45)

Here, and in Obtuse Angle's later denunciation of "Queries," one finds the contempt for rational attempts to find truth ("Idiot Questioning," to Blake) that was evident in many of Blake's subsequent utterances.

The gathering in *An Island in the Moon* contains, as Blake's own social circle probably did, such eighteenth-century types as the scientific virtuoso ("Inflammable Gass the Windfinder") and the Antiquarian. And an enthusiastic preacher is described: "Ah, Mr. Huffcap would kick the bottom of the Pulpit out with Passion-would tear off the sleeve of his Gown & set his wig on fire & throw it at the people. He'd cry & stamp & kick & sweat, and all for the good of their souls" (*CW*, 48). Mr. Huffcap is admired by a good Evangelical lady named Mrs. Sistagatist (possibly Mrs. Mathew): "'Oh!' said Mrs. Sistagatist.' If it was not for churches & chapels I should not have liv'd so long. There was I, up in a Morning at four o'clock, when I was a Girl. I would run like the dickins till I was all in a heat. I would stand till I was ready to sink into the earth'" (*CW*, 48).

Blake himself is present as Quid the Cynic, and he drops hints about his methods as an engraver. (Flaxman is there too, many readers feel, as "Steelyard the Lawgiver.") But the most interesting feature of the work for most readers is the inclusion of the first draft of Blake's fine poem "Holy Thursday," which is offered as a song—and without irony[19]—by Obtuse Angle. Included as well are early versions of "Nurse's Song" and "The Little Boy Lost" which are used to evoke the powerful moods of childhood and thereby to create "good humour." (All three poems were later published in *Songs of Innocence*.)

Receiving a small inheritance resulting from his father's death in July 1784, Blake seemed willing to try the life of the small shopkeeper into which he had been born. With James Parker, another former apprentice of James Basire, Blake opened a small printshop next door to the house of his birth on Broad Street. As was the case whenever Blake violated his instincts in order to serve "Fashion," however, the enterprise did not succeed. But this was the period of Blake's valuable association with his favorite brother, Robert, who was a boy in his teens but already capable of sketches "characterized by Blake-like feeling and intention" (Gilchrist, 1, 57). Robert was to die before he could fulfill his promise as an artist:

> Blake affectionately tended him in his illness, and during the last fort-night of it watched continuously day and night by his bedside, without sleep. When all claim had ceased with that brother's last breath, his own exhaustion showed itself in an unbroken sleep of three days' and nights' duration. The mean room of sickness had been to the spiritual man, as to him most scenes were, a place of vision and revelation; for Heaven lay about him still, in manhood, as in infancy it "lies about us" all. At the last solemn moment, the visionary eyes beheld the released spirit ascend heav-enward through the matter-of-fact ceiling, "clapping its hands for joy." (Gilchrist, 1, 59)

It seems that the visionary eye that saw the significance of his broth-er's death would never lose touch with Robert's genius: "Down to late age the survivor talked much and often of that dear brother; and in hours of solitude and inspiration his form would appear and speak to the poet in consolatory dream, in warning or helpful vision" (Gilchrist, 1, 68). Blake's characteristic method of illuminated printing, the method to be used to publish his poetry and its complementary illustration, was revealed to him by Robert in a dream: "In a vision of the night, the form of Robert stood before him . . . directing him to the technical mode by which could be produced a facsimile of song and design" (Gilchrist, 1, 69). The first of Blake's productions in this mode were to be his tractates in defense of vision and inspiration, *There Is No Natural Religion* and *All Religions Are One* (both 1788).

Swedenborgianism and Revolution

In April 1789, after Blake had made known his views about Deism and about perception in *There Is No Natural Religion* and *All Religions Are One*, William and Catherine were drawn to a meeting held by readers of

Swedenborg to discuss the founding of a New Church. Many Swedenborgians, most notably T. Hartley and John Clowes, the translators of Swedenborg's works into English, found it unnecessary to leave the Church of England, and Swedenborg had been like Wesley in not wishing to found a new sect. As early as 1779, a "Mr. William Blake" had been among the subscribers for the publication of the *Discourses* of the Reverend Jacob Duché, a nonseparatist Swedenborgian well-grounded in Boehme and Law who preached at the Female Orphans Asylum in Lambeth from 1779 until 1792. The Blakes were certainly influenced in their decision to move to Lambeth, to this exact neighborhood of the asylum, by Duché's presence there. The Swedenborgians who issued the call to a gathering at a public house on 13 April 1789—the Blakes not named among them—found that the existing churches were too deeply tainted by what Blake had already attacked as natural religion:

> The Old Church . . . believes that nature is God.
> The Old Church faith should be abolished.
> While the Old Church lasts, Heaven cannot come to man.[20]

Although he would be writing against certain of Swedenborg's views within about a year, Blake signed the list of 32 resolutions passed at the meeting, as did Catherine.[21] Blake's brief flirtation with the Swedenborgian New Church was understandable in someone who had grown up with the Evangelical movement. In the determination of the assembled Swedenborgians to replace faith "directed to a God invisible and incomprehensible,"[22] the Evangelical need for "personal dealings with . . . God and Saviour" can be detected. The visionary Swedenborg not only had valued the "Inner Life," to return to Gladstone's remark yet again, but had also constructed his own science of correspondences "between the seen and the unseen." Blake's good friend John Flaxman joined the New Church, but Blake was inclined to be critical of anyone who willingly became a "Sectary" (*CW,* 77). Blake was, moreover, soon to discover Swedenborg's limits—his abhorrent views on predestination and his conventional moral notions—and thus refuse Swedenborg his discipleship.

Although he retained a respect for aspects of Swedenborg throughout his life, Blake was capable of reaching his own understanding of Christian theology. His friend William Sharp was, by contrast, an enrolled disciple first of Emanuel Swedenborg and then of Joanna Southcott, who promised to give birth to the Saviour. The Church of

England was still corrupted by Natural Theology and was an instrument of an undemocratic state, but with the rise of the Evangelicals changes were occurring. Intellectual fads and new sects were everywhere, but Blake's intellectual independence made him much more difficult to influence than some of his close associates. From Swedenborg, Blake drew vocabulary and some concepts; but he was never one to be "enslav'd by another Man's" (*CW,* 629) system, no matter how much of the Inner Light it might have.

The year of Blake's participation in the Swedenborgian meeting, 1789, was also the year that saw the initial polarization of views in response to the event that would most influence British intellectual and political life in the nineteenth century—the revolution in France. The Unitarian Dr. Richard Price gave a sermon in the Old Jewry that greeted the revolution as little short of the prelude to the Apocalypse ("I could almost say, 'Lord, now lettest thou thy servant depart in peace, for mine eyes have seen thy salvation.' . . . I have lived to see thirty millions of people, indignant and resolute, spurning at slavery, and demanding liberty with an irresistible voice."[23]). Edmund Burke's reply in defense of the Old Order initiated the debate on the French Revolution that found Blake in the camp of the Deist Thomas Paine and the Atheist William Godwin.

For Blake, Paine and Godwin were perhaps strange comrades-in-arms: he criticized Paine's ideas in *A Vision of the Last Judgment* and personally disliked Godwin. We have no reason to think that Blake had anything in common with them other than support of the same class in French politics. Paine's *Rights of Man,* Godwin's *Political Justice,* and Blake's *French Revolution* (set up in proof and bearing the imprint of Joseph Johnson, but never published) were all replies to Burke in defense of the principles of the Revolution. As we shall subsequently see, Blake's treatment of the Revolution differs markedly from that of the others in his characteristically viewing its events as the beginning of a movement toward the perfect liberty that the return to Eternity represents to him.

Lambeth, Felpham, and the Treason Trial

After leaving the Broad Street shop, the Blakes lived from 1785 to 1790 in Poland Street and from 1790 to 1800 at 13 Hercules Buildings, Lambeth, in the neighborhood of Lambeth Palace. Blake had already written the *Songs of Innocence,* demonstrating the transforming power that the innocent eye possesses, before moving from Poland Street, where, as

Stanley Gardner (Gardner 1986) has demonstrated, the enlightened policies of the parish charity school gave Blake hope for a Church and State that would value Innocence properly. In Lambeth he wrote almost all of the writings for which he is best known, with the exception of the epics *Milton* and *Jerusalem*. Here he wrote the *Songs of Experience,* which, by revealing the institutional, moral, and mental restraints under which humanity exists, point the way to the Eternity that authenticates the innocent's intuitions. These poems he engraved, together with *Innocence,* as the fully coherent *Songs of Innocence and Experience* (1794).

In the same year, he treated the psychological damage inflicted by a restrictive moral code in *Visions of the Daughters of Albion*; he gave the fall from the freedom of Eternity a mythic treatment in *The Book of Urizen*; and he continued his anatomy of that process in *The Book of Ahania* and *The Book of Los* the following year. About 1796 he began a long struggle to give the psychological processes of this fall epic expression in *The Four Zoas,* called *Vala* in an earlier form, a work to which he returned from time to time until about 1807, but which he did not engrave. *Europe* (1794) was an even earlier try at the psychological themes of *The Four Zoas*; and *The Four Zoas* was itself to be Blake's quarry for materials to be used in the later epics *Milton* and *Jerusalem.*

In Lambeth, Blake had some success as an engraver and illustrator of the works of others, although his fine illustrations for Edward Young's *Night Thoughts* (1797) were not well received, and the engravings for John Gabriel Stedman's *Narrative of a Five Years' Expedition against the Revolted Negroes of Surinam* that Blake, in his own abhorrence of slavery, had been prompt to complete in 1791 were not to be seen by the public until Joseph Johnson finally published Stedman's book in 1796. Personal details are scarce for the Lambeth period, just as they are for almost every period of Blake's life. What we see in such letters and contemporary references as do exist are once again largely the concerns of a trade and a class. Blake's writings themselves tell us much about his mental life, however, and the few anecdotes about him that survive from this period seem to be in character.

Catherine and he celebrated the Eden-like character of their garden in Lambeth by sitting in the nude in it while reading *Paradise Lost* aloud. (Nudism was in vogue in some London intellectual circles of the time; one of Blake's artistic principles was that "Art can never exist without Naked Beauty displayed" [*CW,* 776].) In Soho a few years earlier, Blake had intervened, at the risk of his own neck, in a street incident in which a man was beating a woman with a cudgel (BR, 31). In Lambeth, he was enraged to find that the owner of a local circus had as a punishment tethered a boy by tying a log to his foot as one would to an animal: Blake's fury in this instance nearly involved him in a fistfight with the circus impresario, but Blake ultimately persuaded him that such disciplinary methods were unjust and inhumane (*BR*, 521–22).

At the end of the Lambeth period, Blake acquired a patron, William Hayley, and the Blakes moved to a cottage at Felpham, a seaside village in Sussex near Chichester, made available by Hayley, who lived nearby. But Hayley's fondness for "the good Enthusiastic Blake"[24] brought with it no understanding of Blake's goals as an artist and as a poet. Finally, in 1803, weary of his patron's "Genteel Ignorance & Polite Disapprobation" (*CW*, 825), Blake knew that he had to return to London. Before he could leave, however, the most dramatic event in Blake's corporeal life occurred.

On 12 August 1802, Blake found a soldier named John Scolfield in his garden, probably invited there by a gardener but without Blake's knowledge; Blake asked him to leave. Scolfield refused, became abusive, and forced Blake to push him from the garden and then 50 yards up the road to the inn where the soldiers were barracked. Scolfield had Blake brought to trial for sedition, alleging that Blake had "*damned the King & said the———Soldiers were all Slaves*" (*BR*, 125). There can be no doubting that, whether Blake said what Scolfield ascribed to him or not, Blake's republican sentiments would be accurately reflected in the remark—but, with the aid of an able attorney named Samuel Rose, Blake was acquitted when his case came to trial in January 1804. The indictment itself is, however, a vivid reminder of the times in which Blake lived. The fears engendered by the events of the French Revolution had cost English people many of their traditional liberties and had produced networks of government spies: apparently the soldier Scolfield sought to take advantage of the temper of the times to soothe his wounded pride.

The Unregarded Prophet

When Blake had again settled down to work in London, his freedom from Hayley's interference and his exhilaration at escaping Scolfield's net led to a burst of creativity that included his starting work on *Milton* and *Jerusalem*; the completion of either was, however, to be years away. He felt, he said after a visit to a collection of pictures exhibited by Joseph,

Count Truchsess, "enlightened with the light I enjoyed in my youth," adding "I am really drunk with intellectual vision" (*CW*, 852). Blake continued, however, to meet with every sort of frustration in his own work as a painter and an engraver. Symptomatic of his experiences in the later years was his attempt to gain some recognition—and to interest the public in his idea of portable frescoes that could be changed from time to time in England's public buildings—by holding an exhibition of his work at 28 Broad Street, the place of his birth and now the hosiery shop of his brother James.

Although Blake displayed works that are now priceless and that are in the great museums and private collections of the world, and although he offered as a guidebook to the exhibition the sourcebook of his ideas, *A Descriptive Catalogue*, he had small success with the show. Worst of all, however, was the response of the exhibition's one reviewer, Robert Hunt, who regarded Blake's efforts as "fresh proof of the alarming increase of the effects of insanity" (*BR*, 215). Hunt had attacked Blake's work before, probably because, as G. E. Bentley, Jr., observes, he "saw him as an enthusiast, if not a Methodist" (*BR*, 197). But that the one public voice raised by Blake's exhibition should be that of an old enemy could only confirm Blake in his decision to accept henceforth his obscurity. Indeed, Blake had already said of himself, "I am hid" (*CW*, 445).

The years that followed the exhibition of 1809 brought Blake's then-unrecognized crowning achievements: the publication of the illustrations to the Book of Job (1826) and the completion in illuminated printing of *Milton* (c. 1810) and of *Jerusalem* (c. 1820). These epic works invited England to embrace a new theology that was based not on a restrictive moral code but on the forgiveness of sins and that had its source in the imagination, which was Jesus present in every man. For those who wished to see Blake as their favorite madman, as H. Crabb Robinson wished to see him, he was willing to veil his comments on vision in a way calculated to entertain his auditor. We now see Blake's conversations with Robinson for the complex teasing of the naive interrogator that they really are.[25] At least Blake had Catherine's company and understanding, and he had also passed beyond wanting material success:

> I have Mental joy & Mental Health
> And Mental Friends & Mental wealth;
> I've a Wife I love & that loves me;

> I've all But Riches Bodily.
>
> I am in God's presence night & day,
>
> And he never turns his face away. (*CW*, 558)

The Blakes now lived in poor rooms in Fountain Court in the Strand that were rented from Catherine's sister; Blake's clothes were "threadbare, and his grey trousers had worn black and shiny in front, like a mechanic's" (*BR*, 281); a Royal Academician was so embarrassed when he saw Blake, who had no servant, carrying home beer himself to accompany the Blakes' dinner that he did not acknowledge him (*BR*, 307).

Blake had the patronage of a government clerk named Thomas Butts and the admiration of a few fellow artists to sustain him in the final period of his life. These last years seem to have been peaceful and cheerful and to have been made that way by his certainty of the truth of his vision and by his awareness of what he had indeed accomplished in his art despite lack of recognition. His attitude as he was dying on 12 August 1827, is in character: "Just before he died his Countenance became fair, his eyes brightened, and he burst out into singing of the things he saw in heaven."[26] Because he had "ever professed his preference of the Church to any sort of sectarianism" (Gilchrist 1, 330), Blake asked for burial in the Church of England: "A little before his death, Mrs. Blake asked where he would be buried, and whether a dissenting minister or a clergyman of the Church of England should read the service. To which he answered that 'as far as his own feelings were concerned, they might bury him where she pleased.' But that as 'father, mother, aunt, and brother were buried in Bunhill-row, perhaps it would be better to lie *there*. As to service, he should wish for that of the Church of England" (Gilchrist, 1, 361).

Catherine Blake followed William to Bunhill Fields on October 20, 1831; but this "estimable woman . . . saw Blake frequently after his decease: he used to come and sit with her two or three hours every day."[27] Clearly, Catherine Blake was like William in her ability to see "through the eye and not with it"—to prefer what the imagination experiences to that which the rational mind tells us we must accept—the same preference that Blake's genius may yet teach much of humankind.

Chapter Two

Poetry and Perception: The Two Tracts on Religion and *The Book of Urizen*

Allegory address'd to the Intellectual powers, while it is altogether hidden from the Corporeal Understanding, is My Definition of the Most Sublime Poetry.

—Letter to Thomas Butts, 6 July 1803

If the Spectator could Enter into these Images in his Imagination, approaching them on the Fiery Chariot of his Contemplative Thought . . . then would he arise from his Grave, then would he meet the Lord in the Air & then he would be happy.

—*A Vision of the Last Judgment*

Poetry in Illuminated Printing

The works that William Blake offered to the unreceptive public of his day are a unique combination of the arts of printmaking and poetry. In works such as *The Book of Urizen* or *Visions of the Daughters of Albion,* each page contains both a portion of the poem's text—in many cases, only a few lines—and a fully colored engraved drawing that either illustrates the text or otherwise complements it. (There are also full-page illustrations between pages with text.) Some of Blake's poems survive in forms other than those represented by the engraved works—*Poetical Sketches,* for example, was printed in the conventional manner as an unillustrated book of poems; *The French Revolution* exists only in the form of the publisher's proof sheets and lacks illustration; and several poems, including the magnificent *Four Zoas,* were left in manuscript by Blake and not engraved.

Works such as these can be represented in print with varying degrees of accuracy, as can Blake's letters and miscellaneous prose. But the character of the engraved works, to which Blake's greatest efforts were devoted, cannot be represented accurately in any conventional printed text. In fact, it has only recently been technically possible to produce first-rate color reproductions of the engraved work. A breakthrough in their availability occurred with the appearance of the Trianon Press facsimiles of Blake's illuminated work, published by the William Blake Trust under the guidance of Sir Geoffrey Keynes; yet few readers were able to see these beautiful editions except in the rare-book rooms of libraries. A revolution in electronic techniques has produced many good full-color editions over the last few years, and *The Illuminated Books of William Blake,* in several volumes, from Princeton University Press in association with the William Blake Trust under the general editorship of David Bindman, is the definitive edition.

In producing a work in illuminated printing, Blake wrote the lines of his poem and drew the accompanying pictures on copper plates. He used acid to etch the areas of the plate surrounding his lettering and the lines of his drawing. The result was a plate that could be used in printing at least the all-important outlines of his work. Blake still had to color the reproduced page by hand, varying the colors from one copy to the next, and often shifting the order of the plates.[1] The fact that the sequence of plates could be changed is one of the unique characteristics of Blake's methods as a narrative poet. It suggests that the individual plates have greater significance in themselves than has the overall narrative ordering of the poem. To understand what led Blake to value the plate above sequential narrative, we must turn to two early prose tracts that also serve as a helpful introduction to Blake's thought.

There Is No Natural Religion and *All Religions Are One*

In *There Is No Natural Religion* (1788), Blake announced his opposition to the dominant British empirical school of philosophy. The reliance on sense experience that had characterized the thought of John Locke and the respect for experiment that had started in England with Francis Bacon had led in the eighteenth century to a philosophy that admitted no truth from sources other than the world of objects that we occupy and our reasonings upon that world. The result of this attitude was the assertion that there exists a "natural religion," a Christianity supported by logic and the observation of "nature" (which was considered to exist independently of the human observer).

For William Blake, there is no natural religion because the theory of knowledge that supports such systems produces not insight into divinity but a sense of imprisonment within an inhuman and inimical universe made of the all-enclosing circles described by a Newton. In *There Is No Natural Religion* (first series, written in 1788), Blake argues that, if we have knowledge only from the senses, we can only identify "objects of sense" as what we desire:

> Man's desires are limited by his perceptions, none can desire what he has not perceiv'd.
>   The desires & perceptions of man, untaught by any thing but organs of sense, must be limited to objects of sense. (*CW*, 97)

How can sense experience produce religious knowledge, Blake asks, when sense experience does not even lead us to *ask* for religious knowledge? All that "sense" produces is an enclosed, inhuman world: "*Conclusion.* If it were not for the Poetic or Prophetic character the Philosophic & Experimental would soon be at the ratio of all things, & stand still, unable to do other than repeat the same dull round over again" (*CW*, 97).

Sense experience leads us to an acceptance of *ratio*, the lowest common denominator picture of the world that "common sense" takes for granted. Such a world offers no hint of possible divinity, and no guidance in conduct either. But, since there is another faculty in humanity, a human being is not "only a natural organ subject to Sense" but possesses what Blake here calls the poetic or prophetic character and what he elsewhere calls the poetic genius or the imagination. As Blake explains later in his commentary on his lost painting *The Vision of the Last Judgment,* he personally rejects the "ratio" way of perceiving for the poetic and imaginative: "'What,' it will be Quest on'd, 'When the Sun rises, do you not see a round disk of fire somewhat like a Guinea?' O no, no, I see an Innumerable company of the Heavenly host crying 'Holy, Holy, Holy is the Lord God Almighty.' I question not my Corporeal or Vegetative Eye any more than I would Question a Window concerning a Sight. I look thro' it & not with it" (*CW*, 617). What one perceives as a "natural organ subject to Sense" is of no more interest than is the window that we look out of: what we must attend to is what the imagination sees. Until we learn to value imaginative perception above "natural" perception, we receive no information at all about what is really important to humans.

In *There Is No Natural Religion* (second series, probably also written in 1788), Blake turns from an attack on eighteenth-century empiricism to an assertion of the powers of the imagination by which a human being "perceives more than sense (tho' ever so acute) can discover." Because empiricism allows itself only the world of the senses, it condemns itself to imprisonment in the physical world: "The bounded is loathed by its possessor. The same dull round, even of a universe, would soon become a mill with complicated wheels" (*CW,* 97). We are trapped, our senses say, in a mill—a grim, revolving machine in which the planets spin coldly in complicated circles. This is the universe that we choose, even though "the bounded is loathed by its possessor," when we accept "ratio" perception. And what we see is really ourselves since we acquiesce in what the universe seems to be: "*Application.* He who sees the Infinite in all things, sees God. He who sees the Ratio only, sees himself only" (*CW,* 98).

In the acts of the imagination, however, "God becomes as we are" because the imagination is divine. If we will be imaginative, rather than ratio-bound, then "we may be as [God] is." God exists not in the natural world to which natural religionists apply their reason but in each of us and in the imagination itself. "This world of Imagination," Blake writes elsewhere, "is the world of Eternity; it is the divine bosom into which we shall all go after the death of the Vegetated body" (*CW,* 605). In fact, even the natural world itself is, in a way, an imaginative creation, although we have frozen it into the cold mill that the ratio sees: "All Things are comprehended in their Eternal Forms in . . . the Human Imagination" (*CW,* 605–6). But the imagination is also "the divine body of the Saviour, the true Vine of Eternity" (*CW,* 606). The healthy human imagination is Jesus. When our perception becomes fully imaginative, the mill-universe ceases to imprison us, and we are once again with Him in Eternity.

In *All Religions Are One,* Blake again argues that all religious knowledge comes, of course, from the divine imaginative faculty. "The true Man is the source, he being the Poetic Genius." The "true Man," the real human being, is any imaginative human who has sought and won freedom from the bounded universe of the senses and is thus free to offer prophecy from the imagination: "*Principle 1st.* That the Poetic Genius is the true Man, and that the body or outward form of Man is derived from the Poetic Genius" (*CW,* 98). Our perception of our own bodies, like our perception of the universe, is the acceptance of a frozen imaginative act. Similarly, every religion is an authentic imaginative creation distorted only by the limits to vision that each prophet has accepted—such as the character of the physical world that the prophet chooses to inhabit or the nature of the civilization that the prophet inherits. Thus, all religions are one because they "have one source," the divine and eternal imagination.

As Minna Doskow has recognized, the fundamental philosophic enterprise of Blake and Marx is similar: "They propose a human definition of man and his world, for both believe that the world has no meaning isolated from man," and they therefore recognize "an extension of the subject outward through consciousness and activity thereby creating a humanized universe as well as a fully developed self" (Doskow 1982a, 225). Both Blake and Marx deny either meaning or independent existence to the separate "external" world that tyrannizes over the minds of empiricists and natural religionists. For Marx, such "nature fixed in isolation from man—is *nothing* for man," but "nature is man's *inorganic* body"[2]; for Blake, "Where man is not, nature is barren" (*CW*, 152). Thus, God must not be sought in a separate world "out there" or "up there" but in ourselves, the creators of the reality that we experience. (Blake: "Thus men forgot that All deities reside in the human breast" [*CW*, 153].) For both Blake and Marx, imagination is the agent in the creation of human reality. As Marx wrote in *Capital:* "What distinguishes the worst architect from the best of bees is this, that the architect raises his structure in imagination before he erects it in reality. At the end of every labour-process, we get a result that already existed in the imagination of the labourer at its commencement" (*M-E*, 344–45). Blake's Evangelical vocabulary names this true Creator as Jesus, as the Divine Humanity in each of us. Their understanding of "the relation of human subjectivity to the external world"—that is, the so-called external world of the empiricist—is the same.

It is important to recognize at this point that Blake seeks to explain, as does Marx, that reality comprises *both* what we designate "subject" and what we designate "object." A fixed physical world independent of the human participant has no reality; but for Blake, as for Marx, human endeavor expresses itself through a material reality in its efforts at a perfected, fully human world, or in its search for what Marx would call "beauty" (*M-E*, 76). If Blake distinguishes himself from the advocates of natural religion in avoiding the dictation from a falsely perceived "nature," he also, like Marx, avoids the trap of idealism, the belief that mind can operate without materials. As an artist, Blake would be more immune from this error than most: indeed he stresses the point that the art work only begins to come into being when one begins physically to draw the defining outlines.

Idealism is not the contrary to the materialism of the simple-minded empiricist because it is simply an arrival at the *same* error, the separation of subject and object, from the opposite direction. As Lenin explains, however, idealism is no worse a delusion than is crude materialism: "Philosophical idealism is *only* nonsense from the standpoint of crude, simple, metaphysical materialism. From the standpoint of *dialectical* materialism, on the other hand, philosophical idealism is a *one-sided,* exaggerated . . . development . . . of one of the features, aspects, sides, facets of knowledge into an absolute, *divorced* from matter, from nature, apotheosised. Idealism is clerical obscurantism. True. But philosophical idealism is . . . a *road* to clerical obscurantism *through one of the shades* of the infinitely complex *knowledge* (dialectical) of man."[3]

Blake, like Marx, avoids "metaphysics" by attending to reality as actually experienced by humanity. The metaphysical division "materialist/idealist" is in fact, for the human being, a concomitant of that division of labor in which human alienation begins. As Engels puts it, "In the division of labour, man is also divided" (*M-E,* 719). For Marx, Blake, and Lenin, the emergence of what Blake calls "priestcraft" is one of the certain symptoms of the division of human faculties that both metaphysics and commerce bring about. "And clerical obscurantism (= philosophical idealism)," Lenin concludes, "is a *sterile flower* . . . that grows on the living tree of living, fertile, genuine, powerful, omnipotent, objective, absolute, human knowledge." Blake's mythic account of what has gone wrong with our philosophy and civilization will frequently tell a similar story of division away from full humanity.

The Characteristics of Blake's Visionary Mode in Poetry

Because Blake believes that our "natural" perception would only deceive and entrap us, while our imaginative perception can bring us truth and freedom, he tries in all his work as a poet and a painter to give us a world seen not with the eye but through it. One effect of his attempt to offer imaginative vision rather than natural sight is, paradoxically perhaps, a radical simplification of his materials down to what communicates his vision and pays no homage to the deceptive natural world. As a result, conventional landscape all but disappears in his poetry, as do "realistically" portrayed human beings. Whether the poem is a Song of Innocence or *Jerusalem,* "simplification," in this sense, is present; for, as Harold Bloom says, Blake's poems "refuse to seek the visually remembered world."[4] Nonetheless, precisely this sort of simplicity has made Blake difficult for many readers to comprehend, although it is the appropriate mode for a poet who tries to lead us to truths knowable not by sense experience but by the poetic genius or imagination.

Blake's own remarks about art stress the importance of clear outline in painting. The true artist is not interested in reproducing the natural world, the world of the senses, but in communicating his vision by means of sharp, clear lines. In this way, the painter simplifies, as does the poet, by ignoring what the senses cause us to see in order to present what the imagination grasps as reality.

Complaints of Blake's "obscurity" were common even in his own day, but Blake's answer to one such indictment should settle the issue once and for all: "You say that I want somebody to Elucidate my Ideas. But you ought to know that What is Grand is necessarily obscure to Weak men. That which can be made Explicit to the Idiot is not worth my care. The wisest of the Ancients considered what is not too Explicit as the fittest for Instruction, because it rouzes the faculties to act" (*CW,* 793). Blake's poetry and his drawings are instruction in vision. Their existence "rouzes the faculties to act" because they are addressed to "the intellectual powers" and not to "the corporeal understanding" that needs, even in art, a recognizable natural world as a crutch. Blake invites us to make the effort to share his vision as it exists in its radical, imaginative simplicity.

Since the source of Blake's vision is the eternal imagination, he holds out the promise that, when he pictures Eternity, we can arise from the "grave" of our lives and "be happy" if we can "enter into these images." In Marxist terms, such human fulfillment would be possible because Blake's "Eternity" clearly involves a release from the alienation that we suffer in a society constituted like ours; for either Marxist or Blakist, it would mean entry into a realm of freedom in which the fundamental human force of imagination operates without restraints; for the Evangelical Blake, it would be a return to Paradise that the Christian awaits. But most often Blake's visionary simplicity is applied not to these final outcomes but to letting us see the truth of our present but mistaken mental states. Blake, looking *through* the eye and not *with* it, sees into our condition and reduces it to the meaningful, clear outlines that he then addresses to our "intellectual powers." To achieve these descriptions of perception, fallen or fulfilled, Blake uses the plate as his unit. Unlike traditional narratives, his epic poems reveal their patterns of meaning not exclusively at the end but constantly, plate by plate.[5]

As Northrop Frye says, in the conventional narrative "theme" is "the narrative seen as total design"; but in Blake's work there is an "elimination of narrative movement" and "the device of a sequence of plates is consistent with the whole scheme."[6] The plates can in fact be shifted without great concern for a narrative structure. As S. Foster Damon has said of Blake's shifting plates in *The Book of Urizen,* "the 'states' which they represent are eternal, and therefore continually happening everywhere."[7] Each plate represents a mode of vision, good or bad, and it invites our intellectual powers to apprehend and evaluate it. If readers of Blake keep this fact in mind, they can overcome much of the frustration that some have felt as a result of what they consider to be narrative confusion or repetition. Blake is writing epics without narrative, but they have significance that can be apprehended plate by plate as our modes of vision encounter those that he depicts. Writing about Blake's epic *Jerusalem,* Minna Doskow explains that "Blake replaces chronological or linear development with a tight thematic unity. Time is transcended as one action is consecutively revealed in all its multiple meanings, from many perspectives."[8] The resulting structure of a Blake narrative is, as Doskow usefully says, "kaleidoscopic."

In defining modes of perception in the poetic portion of his plate, Blake turns to myth. He rarely, however, uses as Milton did any conventional figures from Classical or Christian myth; he invents his own figures, particularly Urizen, Los, Orc, Albion, Jerusalem, Vala, and others of considerable importance. The relationships between these figures have the same function as do any of Blake's drawings for his illuminated printing: they provide the clear outlines that define particular modes of vision. The figures must be self-defining rather than traditionally identifiable because their function requires that they be apprehended immediately by our "intellectual powers" rather than identified through our use of memory or other aspects of the "corporeal understanding."

The Book of Urizen

The best work to introduce the reader to Blake's mythic figures and narrative method is *The Book of Urizen* (1794), a work that is concerned most directly with the problem of the limits that we place on our perception in our acceptance of the natural world. The events in *The Book of Urizen* are a "history" that we reenact every time that we look at the world and see the ratio rather than the infinite: it is Urizen's fall that we participate daily with our unimaginative looking. However the plates are arranged,[9] our vision darkens as we move through *The Book of Urizen* to repeat the fall of the human imaginative powers.

The title page of *The Book of Urizen* pictures an old man, with what are apparently blind eyes, writing with both hands. Behind him stand the stone tablets of the Ten Commandments, and he is enclosed within a series of semicircular forms. The old man is Urizen, whose book this is, and he is one of Blake's most important mythic figures. The name "Urizen" is undoubtedly a pun on "Your Reason," but many readers also find a hint of the word "horizon," with its suggestion of limitations set on vision or indeed of the Greek original of "horizon," οὑριζειν, which means "to limit," an activity that is psychologically necessary to Urizen.[10]

The poem's "Preludium" suggests that Urizen is "the primeval Priest" and the source of a "religion" that is spurned by the Eternals who dictate the poem to Blake. We recognize here that the word *Eternals* is simply another synonym for the imagination, the source of all truth for Blake, and we may also think of the Eternals as an unalienated humanity. Thus we know that Urizen's "religion," whatever it might be, is unimaginative and is, therefore, as suspect as is natural religion.

Chapter 1 begins with the appearance of an ominous force in Eternity:

> Lo, a shadow of horror is risen
> In Eternity! Unknown, unprolific,
> Self-clos'd, all-repelling: what Demon
> Hath form'd this abominable void,
> This soul-shuddering vacuum? Some said
> "It is Urizen." But unknown, abstracted,
> Brooding, secret, the dark power hid. (*CW,* 222)

There is no recognizable landscape because these events occur in Eternity prior to the coming into existence of the limited physical world that humans know. Only mental states are described because they are the source of our delusions about the kind of world we inhabit.

Urizen is mysterious, unproductive, and self-contemplating rather than open and creative. From such secrecy and introversion, which precede what we call "the existence of matter," there arises the fundamental error in our perception. The falling Urizen (like our falling perception) defines and accepts limits:

> Times on times he divided & measur'd
> Space by space in his ninefold darkness,
> Unseen, unknown. (*CW,* 222)

We know Urizen best through his mental attitudes. He is "Your Reason" in all its inadequacy—despite its presumption of primacy in the makeup of a human being. He is the faculty that respects ratio.

"The Eye altering alters all" (*CW,* 426), Blake says elsewhere. And, once Urizen's mental condition is made known, his angle of vision defined, a "physical" world begins to find its troubled existence:

> changes appear'd
> Like desolate mountains, rifted furious
> By the black winds of perturbation
>
> For he strove in battles dire,
> In unseen conflictions with shapes
> Bred from his forsaken wilderness
> Of beast, bird, fish, serpent & element,
> Combustion, blast, vapour and cloud.
>
> Dark, revolving in silent activity:
> Unseen in tormenting passions:
> An activity unknown and horrible,
> A self-contemplating shadow,
> In enormous labours occupied.
>
> But Eternals beheld his vast forests;
> Age on ages he lay, clos'd, unknown,
> Brooding shut in the deep; all avoid
> The petrific, abominable chaos. (*CW,* 222–23)

From the perspective of Eternity, which is where an unalienated human-ity would dwell, the activity of Urizen is terribly mistaken and destruc-tive both of genuine order and of the process by which subject and object actually engage in experience. As he begins "creation," Urizen in fact generates chaos, because a world frozen into physical form is a disordering of human perception. Such a world is deathlike, "petrific," rather than flexible, as is Eternity. "Many suppose," Blake writes elsewhere, "that before the Creation All was Solitude & Chaos. This is the most pernicious Idea that can enter the Mind" (*CW,* 614). Eternity is an active and energetic place; chaos is the "created" world.

We see now why *The Book of Urizen* is sometimes considered Blake's "Book of Genesis." What Urizen is doing is acting as a creator God, but he does so only because of his diseased mental condition—"unprolific," "self-closed," "abstracted," "secret"—and he is that faculty in us that repeats this same false creative process every time we see a fixed physical world around us. Blake effectively communicates the horror of our condition with his adjectives "petrific" and "abominable" and in what follows:

> His cold horrors silent, dark Urizen
> Prepar'd; his ten thousands of thunders,
> Rang'd in gloom'd array, stretch out across
> The dread world; & the rolling of wheels,
> As of swelling seas, sound in his clouds,
> In his hills of stor'd snows, in his mountains
> Of hail & ice; voices of terror
> Are heard, like thunders of autumn
> When the cloud blazes over the harvests. (*CW,* 223)

Such grim facts of physical existence as winter weather ("cold . . . stor'd snows . . . hail & ice"), turbulent waters ("swelling seas"), and preparations for war are suggested. Such ills are, in their origin, mental realities too—they are brought into being by Urizen's determination to create a universe that is in fact separated from humanity and that is therefore alien and threatening. Chapter 2 of *The Book of Urizen* provides still more information about that aspect of our psychological composition that Urizen represents. Chapter 1 has made it clear that he is all that is uncreative and secretive in us and that he needs, therefore, a ratio world to lean on. He has chosen, the opening of chapter 2 reminds us, the "dim rocks" of the created universe in place of the "all flexible senses" that unfallen humanity, the psychologically whole human being, could have. His philosophical and theological errors only deepen as he ascribes divinity to his unprolific and unimaginative act:

> From the depths of dark solitude, From
> The eternal abode in my holiness,
> Hidden, set apart, in my stern counsels,
> Reserv'd for the days of futurity,
>
> I have sought for a joy without pain,
> For a solid without fluctuation.
> Why will you die, O Eternals?
> Why live in unquenchable burnings? (*CW,* 224)

With comic pomposity ("my holiness"), Urizen assumes the God-like position that humans have mistakenly granted to the rational faculty. Rather than the complex excitement and diversity of Eternity, he wishes for an impossible one-dimensional world with no pain, no flux, no death, no passion; in fact, he desires an Eternity not unlike the Heaven that rational Christianity envisioned in the eighteenth century. In the same way that he has started the creation of the fixed physical world "where nothing was" by turning sickly inward to oppose the creative diversity of Eternity ("First I fought with the fire, consum'd / Inwards into a deep world within: / A void immense"), he now turns inward to find a rigid one-dimensional moral law:

> Here alone I, in books form'd of metals,
> Have written the secrets of wisdom,
> The secrets of dark contemplation.
>
> . . . .
>
> Lo! I unfold my darkness, and on
> This rock place with strong hand the Book
> Of eternal brass, written in my solitude. (*CW,* 224)

Already we have enough experience with Blake to suspect anything that can be described as "secrets . . . secrets . . . dark" that are written in the unhealthy voluntary self-enclosure expressed in "alone . . . my dark-

ness . . . my solitude." Finally, Urizen's insanity results in his assumption
of the role of holy lawgiver:

> Laws of peace, of love, of unity,
> Of pity, compassion, forgiveness;
> Let each chuse one habitation,
> His ancient infinite mansion,
> One command, one joy, one desire,
> One curse, one weight, one measure,
> One King, one God, one Law. (*CW*, 224)

As Urizen's need for uniformity turns into the frenzied chant "*One* command, *one . . . one . . . One . . . one . . . one . . . One . . . one . . . one*," Blake's
skillful presentation allows a characteristic grim humor to emerge to aid
us in recognizing and judging what we see. Even as Urizen has been
revealed as our concept of a creator-God ("I repell'd / The vast waves &
arose on the waters"), he is also the lawgiver God of Mount Sinai. Both
pictures of God are entirely false, Blake would say; they are the result of
our worship of the Urizen-faculty in our psychological makeup.

Because Urizen needs laws, he brings into existence for the first time
"all the seven deadly sins of the soul." His action is a mythic representation of the way in which, from the perspective of both Blake and
Marxism, "man," in the words of David Punter, "abdicates his own
responsibility for moral action by inventing a supernatural origin for the
moral law, which then becomes a force of spiritual and institutional
oppression."[11] Systems of "sin" are also another result of the sort of perception that demands fixity, a corollary to the creation of our stony
world, which continues to take place:

> Eternity roll'd wide apart,
> Wide asunder rolling
> Mountainous all around
> Departing, departing, departing,
> Leaving ruinous fragments of life
> Hanging, frowning cliffs, & all between,
> An ocean of voidness unfathomable. (*CW*, 225)

Urizen tries to find a home in this world, but he cannot until he creates the additional limits that are, because the result of one error, simultaneously our universe, our planet, and our skull:

> And a roof, vast, petrific, around
> On all sides he fram'd like a womb,
> Where thousands of rivers in veins
> Of blood pour down the mountains to cool
> The eternal fires, beating without
> From Eternals; & like a black globe,
> View'd by sons of Eternity standing
> On the shore of the infinite ocean,
> Like a human heart, strugling & beating,
> The vast world of Urizen appear'd. (*CW,* 225–26)

What Urizen has done is to "create" in a manner that satisfies, perhaps, the rational faculty's craving for definites; but, in the process, he has separated himself from the genuine imaginative sources of truth. He has, in fact, repeated the process by which British empirical philosophy created its own mill-universe, the closed world that the mind first creates and then declares the only source of knowledge.

The faculty in the human psychology that Urizen in his assumed sovereignty has thrust aside is imagination, which is represented most nearly in Blake's mythology by Los, who has suffered the loss of Eternity in Urizen's insane wish for restriction rather than for flexibility. Because all that we see is imaginative, the world that Urizen creates is also imaginative; but Urizen has frozen his world into a false fixity. Or, mythically speaking, he has forced Los to make the creation of Urizen seem permanent. With Urizen's choice of the enclosure that is our universe, "Eternity stood wide apart, / As the stars are apart from the earth." The distance of the stars above our heads is immediate evidence of the fashion in which we as "perceivers" have lost possession of our "perception." In *The Four Zoas,* humanity begins a return to Eternity by reaching upward to pull down the moon and the stars. But in *Urizen* Los is forced, "cursing his lot," "to confine / The obscure separation alone"—to confirm Urizen, and humankind, in diseased solipsism.

Urizen is "unorganiz'd" in his demand for fixity because only in Eternity is there a healthy organization that would include a balance in the claims of the different mental faculties. Urizen creates "Death," as the Eternals point out, because he reduces humanity to the status of a "clod of clay." One of Blake's favorite ironies is that those whom we call "the living" are actually "the dead."

Marx, in a portion of *The German Ideology* for which he is considered the primary author, explains that "Division of labour only becomes truly such from the moment when a division of material and mental labour appears." Marx adds a marginal note to his manuscript: "the first form of ideologists, *priests,* is concurrent" (*M-E,* 159). If, as we have seen, Urizen is the "primeval Priest," and therefore in his rationality the first mental worker, then Los is the first material worker. Forced to freeze the products of the imagination, Los struggles in anguished darkness, working as a blacksmith to make permanent Urizen's changes. In the process, he creates time:

> The Eternal Prophet heav'd the dark bellows,
> And turn'd restless the tongs, and the hammer
> Incessant beat, forging chains new & new,
> Numb'ring with links hours, days & years. (*CW,* 227)

With each limitation, the human mind becomes less effective:

> Forgetfulness, dumbness, necessity,
> In chains of the mind locked up,
> Like fetters of ice shrinking together,
> Disorganiz'd, rent from Eternity,
> Los beat on his fetters of iron,
> And heated his furnaces, & pour'd
> Iron sodor and sodor of brass. (*CW,* 228)

As Los hammers out the limitations of humanity, the forms of our physical body emerge. The first part to appear is the head: "a roof, shaggy wild, inclosed / In an orb his fountain of thought" (*CW,* 228). The mental disorder of self-ordained enclosure, presented here in a manner almost comic, materializes into the particular head of a man. The spine, ribs, heart, and stomach follow; and the senses are reduced to the frail and deceptive instruments that we know.

Because our senses are so limited, we no longer have the full, imaginative participation that we had in Eternity before this process of alienation began. Instead, we possess the chaotic sea of sensation:

> All the myriads of Eternity,
> All the wisdom & joy of life
> Roll like a sea around him,
> Except what his little orbs
> Of sight by degrees unfold. (*CW,* 230)

The nightmare of life in the physical world replaces the dynamic and real dreams of Eternity: "And now his eternal life / Like a dream was obliterated."

Los, the representative in us of the poetic genius, accepts what we can now call "the world of the senses." The result is the horror at the vast, inhuman universe that is the historical result of the British empirical tradition:

> Los suffer'd his fires to decay;
> Then he look'd back with anxious desire,
> But the space, undivided by existence,
> Struck horror into his soul. (*CW,* 230)

Los's error is our error in ratio perception. Even though he possesses the power of the imagination, he simply accepts a world "Frozen / Into horrible forms of deformity" that he himself has created. Instead of demanding change, he feels pity, an emotion that is proof of his imaginative weakness because it accepts the world rather than trying to change it:

> He saw Urizen deadly black
> In his chains bound, & Pity began.
>
> In anguish dividing & dividing,
> For pity divides the soul. (*CW,* 230)

The division of the soul of Los produces Enitharmon, the first "female" form; brings the sexes into the world for the first time; and leads toward our kind of existence, which Blake calls "Generation," which has men and women instead of the undivided Divine Humanity. The division of labor was, Marx explains, "originally nothing but the division of labour in the sexual act" (M-E, 158); but here in fact Blake anticipates Marx in seeing our gendered world as one that has left behind a primal unity. Los was the creator of space and time, as we have seen; but, from now, on, Enitharmon represents space and Los time—indeed, Enitharmon is the first of the many female figures that represent roughly "the natural world" that we will encounter. With the birth of Enitharmon and with the additional disintegration of our imaginative powers that she represents, we are separated even more completely from Eternity; the imagination (represented in its unfallen power by the Eternals) cannot learn from nature but risks being stifled by it. The Eternals must refuse to contemplate a world with Enitharmon in it:

> "Spread a Tent with strong curtains around them.
> Let cords & stakes bind in the Void,
> That Eternals may no more behold them."
> They began to weave curtains of darkness,
> They erected large pillars round the Void,
> With golden hooks fasten'd in the pillars;
> With infinite labour the Eternals
> A woof wove, and called it Science. (CW, 231)

What we call "science," a knowledge based on delusive "nature," is not the truth about our existence but that which separates us from the truth. The Newtonian world machine, a "scientific" model of nature that denies imagination a role in perception and separates subject and object, has been completed.

Yet, even in our world of Space and Time, the fallen imagination is often open to Eternity. We still have emotions, and some of us are artists. Thus, even within the natural processes of Generation, which otherwise bind us to the earth, a revolutionary possibility can arise. In chapter 6, which recounts the conception, the life in the womb, and the birth of Orc, we find Blake's usual revolutionary figure and representative of the passionate aspects of our makeup. Orc passes through Generation itself, and his doing so recapitulates what is still considered the scientific history of human evolution:

> Coil'd within Enitharmon's womb
> The serpent grew, casting its scales;
> With sharp pangs the hissings began
> To change to a grating cry:
> Many sorrows and dismal throes,
> Many forms of fish, bird & beast
> Brought forth an Infant form
> Where was a worm before. (*CW,* 232)

Like the serpent in the Garden, Orc threatens change; and, ironically enough, Los and Enitharmon, who hardly need fear the loss of Paradise now, fear the change their offspring represents. Eternity passes seemingly beyond reach as Los accepts the generative cycles. "No more Los beheld Eternity"; instead, he accepts the restrictive patterns of natural life:

> A tightening girdle grew
> Around his bosom. In sobbings
> He burst the girdle in twain;
> But still another girdle
> Oppress'd his bosom. In sobbings
> Again he burst it. Again
> Another girdle succeeds.
> The girdle was form'd by day,
> By night was burst in twain. (*CW,* 233)

Even though the cycle means "sorrow & pain," Los and Enitharmon so fear change that they insist that Orc be as enchained as they are. To enslave him in this way is to force him to worship Urizen, whose "jealous" demand for a world that suits *his* nature created their and our physical world:

> They chain'd his young limbs to the rock
> With the Chain of jealousy
> Beneath Urizen's deathful shadow. (*CW,* 233)

But Orc represents the possibility of revolutionary change. If Los and Enitharmon do not chain him down, if we do not restrain the passionate element in us—that realm of feeling in which our very resentment of our condition creates what contemporary Marxists call the counterhegemonic—revolution will begin that will lead through political change to, finally, a return to Eternity:

> The dead heard the voice of the child
> And began to awake from sleep;
> All things heard the voice of the child
> And began to awake to life. (*CW*, 233)

The dead are what we call the living, and Orc invites them back to Eternity, the only real life. But Orc is restrained again and again—historically, seven times, Blake suggests elsewhere—before the movement back to Eternity can begin.

Urizen's "Science" continues to take shape in the remainder of chapter 7 and in chapter 8. He invents measuring instruments and tries to understand the physical world about him. He invents the scientific modes of understanding such a world; and he even develops the system of the elements when he causes Thiriel (air), Utha (water), Grodna (earth), and Fuzon (fire) to come into existence. But humanity does not respond as well to Urizen's categories as does the inert physical world that he jealously needs: "he curs'd / Both sons & daughters; for he saw / That no flesh nor spirit could keep / His iron laws one moment." He recognizes that his creation is somehow imperfect ("For he saw that life liv'd upon death: / The Ox in the slaughter house moans, / The Dog at the wintry door"); but his response is entirely the wrong one, for "he wept & he called it Pity." From this pity for humanity's failure to satisfy his love of rigidity is invented the theology that would explain such human failure to measure up:

> a Web, dark & cold, throughout all
> The tormented element stretch'd
> From the sorrows of Urizen's soul.
> And the Web is a Female in embrio,
> None could break the Web, no wings of fire,

> So twisted the cords, & so knotted
> The meshes, twisted like to the human brain.

> And all call'd it The Net of Religion. (*CW*, 235)

The web is a "female in embrio" because she is that representative of false religion, the Whore of Babylon, who is called Rahab in Blake's system. But the origin of this web is, of course, the human brain.

With further restrictions, moral and theological, as well as perceptual, in effect for humanity, the human form shrinks even more, as the beginning of chapter 9 explains. Humans create themselves as they place limits on their imagination and passions:

> in reptile forms shrinking together,
> Of seven feet stature they remain'd.

> Six days they shrunk up from existence,
> And on the seventh day they rested,
> And they blessed the seventh day in sick hope,
> And forgot their eternal life. (*CW*, 236)

They bind themselves to the earth, just as Orc was bound:

> No more could they rise at will
> In the infinite void, but bound down
> To earth by their narrowing perceptions
> They lived a period of years;
> Then left a noisom body
> To the jaws of devouring darkness. (*CW*, 236)

They accept death, and they accept Urizen's rigid energy-denying laws:

> And their children wept, & built
> Tombs in the desolate places,
> And form'd laws of prudence, and call'd them
> The eternal laws of God. (*CW*, 236)

Only Fuzon, the destructive element of fire, and therefore similar to the passionate Orc as an aspect of our makeup, remains to suggest the possibility of change. He does not accept this "Egypt," this land of death and captivity, that we accept. But, for now, like Orc, he simply remains the unrealized potentiality of our ultimate return to the joys of Eternity.

The Blakean Myth

The Book of Urizen reveals the outlines of Blake's mythic system. Urizen, Los, Orc, Enitharmon, even Fuzon (and Grodna, Thiriel, and Utha) represent aspects of our own mental life, particularly as it relates to our modes of perception. As literary characters these figures have, of course, no "realistic" appeal at all: they are drawn in the sharp outline form that for Blake constitutes great art, and all accidents of shade are burned away. Nevertheless, Urizen is seen again and again as the white-haired, weeping law giver that we see in the illustrations and text of *The Book of Urizen*. Similarly, Orc remains the dangerous revolutionary boy, and Los continues to represent the spirit of poetry and prophecy that is forced by Urizen to freeze our imaginative world into the delusive forms of ratio perception—but that is still capable of hearing the voices of Eternity and of undertaking the labor of forging that world anew. Los is, despite his fall, nonetheless the imaginative side of us. Imagination, as Marx has explained, is always the human prelude to labor and therefore that propensity for changing the world that constitutes our humanness. Fuzon will merge with the figure of Orc, whom he resembles even here, in much of Blake's later work.

Indeed, the exact history of these mythic figures shifts and is retold with additions and changes, throughout Blake's career. Blake's interest is in what they say about our mental condition and history and is not in any "life" of their own that these figures might possess. For Milton, the exact history of Satan's revolt and Adam's fall was worth establishing; but Blake, who knows what our exact mental history is, feels no need to adhere to a frozen set of imaginative equivalents for it.

But the admission of change into Blake's mythic system does not deny that there are important basic outlines within it. Most of the system is revealed in *The Book of Urizen*; but, since Blake subsequently employs it, it is useful to know that the healthy human personality that we all possessed before Urizen's creation of a fixed world comes to be named Albion in Blake's myth. Blake also accepts Albion as a traditional name for England, so that a restored Albion will also represent a

reborn England. Albion's emanation—the imaginative world that he
and we would inhabit were we not asleep (Albion is often pictured as
sleeping, blind to the Eternity about him)—is named Jerusalem. Thus
Urizen (roughly, reason), Los (imagination), and Orc (passion) come to
represent aspects of Albion's makeup as they represent aspects of our
makeup. In Eternity, we learn as we read on in Blake, these figures had
different names than they have in Generation. Urizen is an eternal name,
but we have so far encountered Los and Orc only after the fall and need
to learn their eternal names. Furthermore, there is a fourth aspect of
Albion and our personality that we encounter only in later tellings of the
myth: his eternal name is Tharmas, and he is representative of the
healthy unity of perception that we once possessed.

A chart of some sort is perhaps useful as we begin to read Blake:

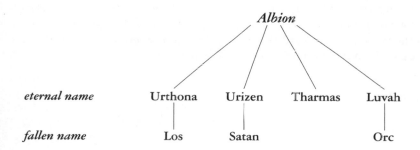

Los is the earth-owner (Urthona) in Eternity because he, and not
Urizen, is the true creator of such imaginative shapes as our fallen perception has frozen into the features of the fallen world. Orc is Luvah
("Lover") in Eternity because there passion has its right name too.
Urizen in his fall, which is to say his creation of the world, is Satan,
whom we all know to be Prince of this world. The four figures—Los,
Orc, Urizen, Tharmas—are called the "four zoas" by Blake because they
remind us of the four figures—eagle, lion, ox, and human—around the
throne of the Lamb in the Book of Revelation (Damon 1971, 458).

The Four Zoas (written 1797–1807) is the most complete working out
of the mythic system suggested by *The Book of Urizen*; but Blake wrote
The Book of Ahania (1795), *The Book of Los* (1795), and *The Song of Los*
(1795) as first attempts at a continuation of *The Book of Urizen*'s story of
the disintegration of the human mind. In 1794, the year of *The Book of
Urizen* itself, Blake also published *Europe,* in which he depicts the domi-

nance that an externalized "nature" and a "natural religion" based on "nature" assert over humankind. These shorter works have the same themes as the epics Blake later wrote, and they confirm what *Urizen* has demonstrated about his mythology and method.

Blake's poetry, lyric or epic, consistently reveals the outlines of this myth, which Blake has devised to show the way out of darkness and restriction:

> I give you the end of a golden string,
> Only wind it into a ball,
> It will lead you in at Heaven's gate
> Built in Jerusalem's wall. (*Jerusalem* [CW, 716])

Under the guidance of the Blakean myth, we begin our movement toward a restored perception, toward psychological health and an end to alienation, and toward the human Eternity where we can, in Blake's exact definition of human need, "be happy."

Chapter Three
Poetical Sketches

Poetical Sketches (1783) collects poems written by Blake in "untutored youth, commenced in his twelfth, and occasionally resumed by the author till his twentieth year" (*CW,* 883). Despite the attempts of some scholars to find a significant correspondence between Blake's fully realized "system," as it appears in the major works of the years to come, and these juvenile experiments in writing verse, it is more accurate to acknowledge, with Stanley Gardner, "how conventional some of the *Poetical Sketches* are." As Gardner recognizes, "Blake wrote later with such uncompromising originality that the ordinariness of the beginning is often forgotten" (Gardner 1968, 32). What any reader of poetry does find, however, are such fine individual lyrics as the unrhymed sonnet "To the Evening Star":

> Thou fair-hair'd angel of the evening,
> Now, while the sun rests on the mountains, light
> Thy bright torch of love; thy radiant crown
> Put on, and smile upon our evening bed!
> Smile on our loves, and, while thou drawest the
> Blue curtains of the sky, scatter thy silver dew
> On every flower that shuts its sweet eyes
> In timely sleep. Let thy west wind sleep on
> The lake; speak silence with thy glimmering eyes,
> And wash the dusk with silver. Soon, full soon,
> Dost thou withdraw; then the wolf rages wide,
> And the lion glares thro' the dun forest:
> The fleeces of our flocks are cover'd with
> Thy sacred dew: protect them with thine influence. (*CW,* 3)

Further, in the longing for a world protected from the fierce wolves and lions that make up physical life, the student of Blake cannot miss the same longing for Eden that is authenticated in the *Songs of Innocence* and that is later given its place in the "system" as an aspect of human need that only Eternity can satisfy. In fact, if one continues to approach *Poetical Sketches* with the intent of seeking a cast of mind that would only subsequently find adequate expression, one can read the poems of Blake's adolescence with some profit and with undiminished pleasure because of what is done well.

The works are imitative, particularly in subject matter, and are often laced with stock eighteenth-century poetic diction. Yet the longing for a transformed world that is fundamental to Blake's as-yet-unembodied vision is in "Song" ("Fresh from the dewy hill" [*CW,* 91]):

> So when she speaks, the voice of Heaven I hear:
> So when we walk, nothing impure comes near;
> Each field seems Eden, and each calm retreat;
> Each village seems the haunt of holy feet.

Similarly, there seems to be, even in Blake's quite conventional addresses to the four seasons, hints of a habit of mind that links an individual's psychology with the type of physical and seasonal environment that person inhabits. In "To Summer" (*CW,* 2), Blake tells us we must possess inspiration and energy to earn summer:

> Our bards are fam'd who strike the silver wire:
> Our youths are bolder than the southern swains:
> Our maidens fairer in the sprightly dance:
> We lack not songs, nor instruments of joy.

The fulfillment that autumn can represent comes in "To Autumn" (*CW,* 2) only when one is artist enough to earn it: "O autumn . . . / . . . tune thy jolly voice to my fresh pipe; / And all the daughters of the year shall dance!" In "To Spring" (*CW,* 1), the earth that we inhabit must deserve spring: "put / Thy golden crown upon her languished head, / Whose modest tresses were bound up for thee!" In "To Winter," that season seems to arrive despite our endeavors; it denies our impulse to participate; but even winter seems to respond to a changed psychological environment: "heaven smiles, and the monster / Is driv'n yelling to his caves beneath mount Hecla" (*CW,* 3).

As Blake's critics have observed, the abstractions in these poems about the seasons are the ancestors of Blake's mythic figures: Winter,

with its life-denying assertion of sovereignty, seems particularly to antic-
ipate Urizen. But most important to the student of Blake is simply the
recognition that his instinctive assumption in these poems is that the
quality of our participation as perceiver is related somehow to the quality of the combined mental and physical environment that we possess.

If we receive the sort of physical environment that we deserve, we certainly make our own artistic environment. Thus the muses absent themselves from England in "To the Muses" *because* "The languid strings do
scarcely move! / The sound is forc'd, the notes are few!" (*CW,* 11). But
the most striking poem in the collection, the one that seems most of all
like the work of the adult Blake, is "Mad Song." In it we find an individual in the mental state that the empirical habits of the eighteenth century would necessarily encourage. His error is the solipsism of a
Urizen—or a Newton; he "infold[s]" his "griefs" and sees a closed, inhuman world:

> Lo! to the vault
> Of paved heaven
> With sorrow fraught
> My notes are driven. (*CW,* 9)

Heaven is "paved" only to someone who chooses to inhabit the world of
ratio vision. Such a person refuses the truth of inspiration and prefers the
darkness that Blake would one day call Ulro:

> After night I do croud,
> And with night will go;
> I turn my back to the east,
> From whence comforts have increas'd;
> For light doth seize my brain
> With frantic pain. (*CW,* 9)

As Blake later recognized, what this world considers as madness in a
poet like Cowper or in Blake himself is "a refuge from unbelief" (*CW,*
772), a refuge from the real madmen, "Bacon, Newton and Locke," or
from anyone who might be the speaker of "Mad Song."

In the instinctive aversion to enclosure within a world whose sky is, in
"Mad Song," "the vault / Of paved heaven," we also find an early exam-

ple of the images of restriction that characterize Blake's portrayal of our
rigid world of physical, political, and moral limitation. Another example
is found in "How sweet I roam'd from field to field," in which Cupid
("the prince of love") captures the speaker in the tender trap of physical
passion:

> He caught me in his silken net,
> And shut me in his golden cage.
>
> He loves to sit and hear me sing,
> Then, laughing, sports and plays with me;
> Then stretches out my golden wing,
> And mocks my loss of liberty. (*CW,* 6)

    Later Blake warns us against the natural heart that ties us to this fall-
en world of our bad perception. Already we find the beginning of
Blake's awareness that "the [visionary] Eye sees more than the Heart
knows" and that imagination must ultimately break the cage into which
the natural heart leads us. Indeed, the prose "Contemplation" printed in
Poetical Sketches has the thoroughly Blakean "I am wrapped in mortality,
my flesh is a prison, my bones are bars of death" (*CW,* 7). The thought is
a usual Christian one, frequently voiced in Blake's time. The future
Bishop of London and supporter of the Evangelicals, Beilby Porteus, had
ended his *Death: A Poetical Essay* (1773) with

> my rapt Soul anticipating Heav'n
> Bursts from the thraldom of incumbring clay,
> And on the wing of Extasy upborn
> Springs into Liberty, and Light, and Life.[1]

But, conventional or not, a view of our present life as in every sense a
prison seems to have been taking shape in Blake's mind from his earliest
days, since we are told that "How sweet I roamed" was written when he
was fourteen.
    Other hints of Blake's future attitudes and interests are found in
"Gwin, King of Norway," in the hatred of tyranny it reveals and in the
apocalyptic imagery that revolution calls forth:

The god of war is drunk with blood;
The earth doth faint and fail;
The stench of blood makes sick the heav'ns;
Ghosts glut the throat of hell!

O what have Kings to answer for,
Before that awful throne!
When thousand deaths for vengeance cry,
And ghosts accusing groan!

Like blazing comets in the sky,
That shake the stars of light,
Which drop like fruit unto [the] earth
Thro' the fierce burning night;

Like these did Gwin and Gordred meet. (*CW,* 13–14)

Furthermore, we are struck by the appearance of Albion as the future home of Liberty in Blake's pseudo-Shakespearean play "King Edward the Third," because we know that, for the mature Blake, "Jerusalem is named Liberty among the Sons of Albion" and that the return of Jerusalem to Albion will be the theme of Blake's last great epic. Perhaps we can even see the mythic giant Albion himself—though still the "she" that it has been traditional to use when speaking of nations—in the fragment called "Prologue to King John": "O yet may Albion smile again, and stretch her peaceful arms, and raise her golden head, exultingly" (*CW,* 34). And when we read in the same brief paragraph that "Tyranny hath stain'd fair Albion's breast with her own children's gore," we think at once of Blake's later assertion that child sacrifice is the inevitable result and a clear sign of the presence of natural religion. But, in such a search for what is Blakean among these pieces of juvenilia, one must look farther and farther into the future to seek points of comparison.

Blake himself seems to have been unwilling to dwell in the past represented by these early productions, for the Reverend A. S. Mathew's apologetic preface tells us that Blake's "talents having been wholly directed to the attainment of excellence in his profession, he has been deprived of the leisure requisite to such a revisal of these sheets, as might have rendered them less unfit to meet the public eye" (*CW*, 883). Many readers take Mathew's remark to mean that Blake did not bother to correct the proofs of his poems. Apparently he made no effort to publish the unbound pages that came from his anonymous printers. Perhaps we are wisest to take the hint and to concentrate upon his adult productions.

Chapter Four

The Marriage of Heaven and Hell

The Theological and Political Context

Even though *The Marriage of Heaven and Hell* (c. 1793) is of particular value to anyone beginning the study of William Blake, it is perhaps unfortunate that this work has come to serve as almost the only one of Blake's, other than a few of his lyrics, that some students ever see. The work is hardly a characteristic production, as it is written largely in prose and contains only minimal poetry, and it is not mythic except in the appended "Song of Liberty" portion. Blake relies in this work on the aphorism and on prose accounts of visionary experiences called "memorable fancies"—Blake's parody of Emanuel Swedenborg's offering "memorable relations" of his visions of Eternity.

Even the attitude toward Swedenborg, whether directly presented or implied in the parodies, does not represent Blake's consistent estimate of Swedenborg's value. Although Blake came to resent Swedenborg's apparent belief in predestination and in a conventional system of moral law, he could still recommend the "works of this visionary" as being "well worthy the attention of Painters and Poets" because they are "foundations for grand things" (*CW*, 581).[1] Blake's thought, his language, and his work in the visual arts were indebted throughout his career to Swedenborg. There is much in the resolutions of the Swedenborgian convention of 1789 that Blake could have subscribed to all his life, even as he did in that year. The mature Blake would have agreed with the young Blake that "all Faith and Worship directed to any other, than to the one God Jesus Christ in his Divine Humanity" is "directed to a God invisible and incomprehensible" (the God that Blake calls "Nobodaddy" in one of his Manuscript Notebook poems). Similarly, Blake would always hold that "immediately on the Death of the material body . . . man rises again to his spiritual or substantial body, wherein he existeth in perfect human form."[2] Blake's habit of speaking of the Divine Humanity and of using the human form as the index of perfection is the most striking result of his exposure to Swedenborg's thought.

Blake's quarrel with Swedenborg in *The Marriage* is, therefore, limited to subsidiary points.[3] Indeed, Blake seems to evince some resentment of Swedenborg's presumption to exclusive possession of visionary powers that see truths not available to the conventionally religious (whom Blake calls the "religious"). Swedenborg "imagines that all are religious, & himself the single one on earth that ever broke a net" (*CW,* 157). The reason for Swedenborg's presumption, Blake feels, is his lack of contact with other energetic visionaries, such as Paracelsus and Jacob Boehme or Dante and Shakespeare: Swedenborg "conversed with Angels who are all religious, & conversed not with Devils who all hate religion" (*CW,* 157).

Not only have visionaries broken nets before, but to Blake in 1790 it seemed that all of Western civilization was breaking nets. The French Revolution was under way, and the revolutionary spark would spread from France to bring political change, of course, but also to restore humanity's fallen perception: "Now is the dominion of Edom [France], & the return of Adam into Paradise" (*CW,* 149). The return of Adam to Paradise, or human entry into the Eternity of unalienated existence, means that humans will repossess and rehumanize the world of "objects" that has been offered us by the philosophy that has served as a prop of the existing political order.

In 1790, Blake is delighted to find himself 33 years old, the age of Christ at the Resurrection. He has himself undergone something of a resurrection, having refused Swedenborg his total allegiance ("Swedenborg is the Angel sitting at the tomb: his writings are the linen clothes folded up" [*CW,* 149]); but he still relishes Swedenborg's having identified the year of Blake's birth as the beginning of the return to Paradise ("a new heaven is begun, and it is now thirty-three years since its advent" [*CW,* 149]). For too long the priest ("the sneaking serpent" who "walks in mild humility"), whose emergence is for both Blake and Marx the symptom of a humanity fragmented in the division of labor, has tyrannized over mental life, while "the just man" who demands a return to an unalienated condition—to Eternity for Blake—"rages in the wilds." Now, in 1790, Blake feels that the rehumanization of France and the resurrection of the spirit that he has himself undergone in transcending the limits of Swedenborg are manifestations of the liberation of human powers repressed by philosophy and society. Energy (meaning both passion and imagination) no longer denied will bring the just man in from the wilds—no matter what fears such a restoration might strike in the hearts of the pious ("the Eternal Hell revives").

Blake's Quarrel with Rational Theology and Morality

Like Urizen, and unlike Blake, Christians of the eighteenth century stressed rules for conduct so strongly that they falsified their own nature. In denying everything that is energetic in themselves and in saying that "Good is the passive that obeys Reason . . . / Evil is the active springing from Energy," they have accepted the theology of a John Milton, who, Blake says, pictures God as "Destiny," Jesus as "a Ratio of the five senses," and the Holy Ghost as "Vacuum." To Blake, such Christians are in religion what Sir Joshua Reynolds is in art—the enemies of inspiration. As the Evangelical clergyman Joseph Milner put it, "Reason . . . has impertinently meddled with the Gospel, and that with such overwhelming sedulity as to darken it more and more."[4] Blake offers some fundamental truths to such Christians:

1. Man has no Body distinct from his Soul; for that call'd Body is a portion of Soul discern'd by the five Senses, the chief inlets of Soul in this age.
2. Energy is the only life, and is from the Body; and Reason is the bound or outward circumference of Energy.
3. Energy is Eternal Delight. (*CW*, 149)

The conventionally religious follow Urizen in his rage for oneness, but the truth is that we are made up of forces in perpetual conflict: reason is good, but only in its function of setting limits for energy. These opposing forces in humankind, both sides of which must be recognized, are called "contraries" by Blake: "Without Contraries is no progression. Attraction and Repulsion, Reason and Energy, Love and Hate, are necessary to Human existence" (*CW*, 149). For a dialectical mind like that of V. I. Lenin, "development is the 'struggle' of opposites" (Lenin, 38, 360); but Blake, writing more than a century before Lenin, invites us to grasp reality in a similarly dialectical way. In Eternity, life would be seen as dynamic and characterized by the opposition of contraries that Blake calls "intellectual War"; but Urizen and most Christians choose our fixed world of fallen perception and of rigid moral categories. Reality is dialectical in nature, and it is situated in the experiencing "Soul," where subject and object engage. Our empirical age relies on the senses to objectify and commodify and in the process to distinguish body from soul. No world exists, however, other than the one situated in human experience, so Blake can be certain there is "no Body distinct from . . . Soul."

Blake's purpose in *The Marriage of Heaven and Hell* is, then, a restoration of energy's rightful place in a world dominated by reason. With such a restoration there will come about a better understanding of the Jesus who is the human imagination. For Blake, Jesus is not the rational law giver of many eighteenth-century Christians; He is "all virtue, and acted from impulse, not rules." In this reevaluation of Jesus, Blake anticipates the direction of much later theology, in which "the 'eschatological' or 'apocalyptic' Jesus emerges . . . hardly the teacher of secular morality."[5] As Blake wittily puts the same point, "If Morality was Christianity, Socrates was the Saviour" (*CW,* 775).

To restore energy, as well as an energetic Jesus, to its rightful place, Blake employs shock tactics based on a reversal of values that makes him the devil's spokesman. In one such reversal, Blake uses the example of the Puritan John Milton, who perhaps wrote his greatest poetry in the speeches of Satan, to show the energetic or "Infernal" origins of poetry: "Note: The reason Milton wrote in fetters when he wrote of Angels & God, and at liberty when of Devils & Hell, is because he was a true Poet and of the Devil's party without knowing it" (*CW,* 150). In order to supply the reader with Blake's own "Infernal wisdom," he interviews conventional angels and energetic devils in the five Memorable Fancies of *The Marriage of Heaven and Hell.* The hells that he visits seem to be places filled with terror to the conventional mind; but Blake walks "among the fires of hell, delighted with the enjoyments of Genius, which to Angels look like torment and insanity."

In the first Memorable Fancy, Blake finds a devil who, with "corroding fires"—in imitation of Blake's methods as an engraver—has inscribed a cliff-face with this crucial sentence: "How do you know but ev'ry Bird that cuts the airy way, / Is an immense world of delight, clos'd by your senses five?" (*CW,* 150). This question places all that Blake has so far said in *The Marriage of Heaven and Hell* within the context of the ideas about the relationship of subject and object that Blake shared with Marx. Perception, as bourgeois empirical philosophy understands it, denies objects the engagement with the subject that they have in that ordinary human experience wherein the only reality resides; the empiricist's perception instead, to use Blake's word, *closes* objects off from the perceiver. The energy of the object—which is of course our human energy—is denied in our desire for the Urizenic fixity that renders a human world inhuman. As we move back toward Eternity, the frozen world opens again, and the particles that make up the physical world (the Spectres of the Dead) come to life to reveal themselves as "human," as products of the divine imagination in each of us. We can start the return to Eternity ourselves by seeing "the world of delight" that is human energy imprisoned in the object.

Blake announces that he has collected "Proverbs of Hell" that "show the nature of Infernal wisdom." In the Proverbs, we are called to a recognition of the value of impulse:

Prudence is a rich, ugly old maid courted by Incapacity.
He who desires but acts not, breeds pestilence.
. . . .
The apple tree never asks the beech how he shall grow;
nor the lion, the horse, how he shall take his prey.
. . . .
Sooner murder an infant in its cradle than nurse unacted desires. (*CW,* 151–52)

The proverbs startle (and sometimes shock) and cause us to ask questions whose answers are instructive. Further reading in Blake shows that in a world in which human impulse would be free of restraint no one would "murder an infant in its cradle." What Blake calls "child sacrifice" is only practiced in an institutional world of the kind we currently occupy. For Blake the institutionalized moral prohibition in fact creates the vice that it condemns: "Prisons are built with stones of Law, Brothels with bricks of Religion" (*CW,* 151).

The Proverbs comment on the inadequacy of our present modes of perception: "The roaring of lions, the howling of wolves, the raging of the stormy sea, and the destructive sword, are portions of eternity, too great for the eye of man" (*CW,* 151). The inhuman natural world that we have created in divorcing subject and object terrifies us with its indifference to the mortality of the perceiving subject. (And at least two great Romantic poems, Wordsworth's "A Slumber Did My Spirit Seal" and Blake's "The Tyger" directly address this feeling.) But the Proverbs also explain that object and subject can be reconciled and nature can be rehumanized. Thus, "a fool sees not the same tree that a wise man sees" because in wisdom we know that "where man is not, nature is barren" (*CW,* 151–52). In some of the Proverbs, Blake asserts the superiority of immediate experiential knowledge (which he might well call "vision") to the formal logic dominant in his age: "What is now proved was once only imagin'd." "Every thing possible to be believ'd is an image of truth" (*CW,* 151–52). As David Punter has observed, what Blake would assert in statements such as these is "not that the world can be disclosed in human shape through a kind of occult perception, but that it is the creation of such a world which is the human task" (Punter, 15).

Meaning, knowledge, and wisdom come about, as Marx too would assert, through the active intervention in the world that occurs in human labor, which in its most fulfilling form we instead call "art." Thus the Proverbs also celebrate imaginative creativity as the way out of time and back into Eternity: "Eternity is in love with the productions of time" (*CW,* 151). Indeed, the "Proverbs of Hell" in their cryptic way contain much of Blake's message in capsule form: restrictive moral laws, oppressive institutions, perception that objectifies and commodifies, and reliance on the rational rather the experiential—all these restrain our imagination and energy and keep us from the truth and the joy that are always within reach.

Cleansing the Gates of Perception

After the "Proverbs of Hell" Blake devotes a full plate (*CW,* 153) to an explanation of the process by which emerged the mistaken concept of the existence of a God dwelling in a world outside of human experience. Early human engagement with the world far from seeing—and thereby producing—cold objects "animated all sensible objects with Gods or Geniuses." But some individuals, making themselves priests in the process, decided to "abstract the mental deities from their objects" and thus "enslav'd the vulgar."

In *The Economic and Philosophic Manuscripts of 1844,* Marx says that "the gods *in the beginning* are not the cause but the effect of man's intellectual confusion" (*M-E,* 79). In *The German Ideology,* he explains that this process was coincident with the division between "material and mental labor": "from now on consciousness is in a position to emancipate itself from the world and to proceed to the formation of 'pure' theory, theology, philosophy, ethics, etc." (*M-E,* 159). Blake would undoubtedly accept Marx's statement that such externalized "gods on their own were never the lords of labor" (*M-E,* 78) but simply a device for enslaving humanity that simultaneously produces priests. The God dwelling in some nonhuman realm from which the priest can receive divine dictates is rejected by Marx, who objects to philosophers who write "as if this 'realm of God' had ever existed anywhere save in the imagination" (*M-E*, 166), and by Blake, who explains, "Thus men forgot that All deities reside in the human breast."

The second Memorable Fancy, which follows, concerns the process of perception and contains a good explanation of what Blake means by seeing *through* the eye rather than *with* it. In this section of *The Marriage*, he converses with the prophets Isaiah and Ezekiel and receives an explanation from Isaiah of what he meant by saying "God spoke" to him: "I saw no God, nor heard any, in a finite organical perception." Blake is careful not to have Isaiah suggest the existence of a separate world "out there" somewhere beyond the human experience that produces the only reality and unites what we falsely categorize as subject and object. God is, for Blake, real—and therefore within human experience—and thus, as David Punter puts it, "divinity is one of man's aspects, just as are matter and energy" (Punter, 125). Isaiah has made it clear that he saw *through* the eye; God seen *with* the eye—like objects seen with the eye—would lack reality. The conversation continues:

Then I asked: "does a firm perswasion that a thing is so, make it so?"

He replied: "All poets believe that it does, & in ages of imagination this firm perswasion removed mountains; but many are not capable of a firm perswasion of any thing." (*CW*, 153)

As Blake said in his annotations to his copy of Berkeley's *Siris*: "Knowledge is not by deduction, but Immediate by Perception or Sense at once. Christ addresses himself to the man, not to his Reason" (*CW*, 774). Thus "firm perswasion" is both the voice of God and the authentic vision that sees through the eye. The great contribution of the prophets of Israel was to teach that "the Poetic Genius . . . was the first principle."

Blake believes that we can possess the visionary powers of Isaiah and Ezekiel if we choose. When we return to vision, "the whole creation will be consumed and appear infinite and holy, whereas it now appears finite & corrupt." For us, because our Urizenic tendency is to restrain the imagination and to repress energy, "This [restoration of infinity] will come to pass by an improvement of sensual enjoyment." Sex is the single imaginative act that most humans can manage at this stage in their history. If we remove the notion "that man has a body distinct from his soul," the sexual act itself becomes proof of the powers of the imagination in humanizing the frozen physical world that seems to surround us. Blake awaits our return to vision:

If the doors of perception were cleansed every thing would appear to man as it is, infinite.

For man has closed himself up, till he sees all things thro' narrow chinks of his cavern. (*CW,* 154)

As the third Memorable Fancy (in which Blakean books are seen being formed in fires and ornamented with jewels) then shows, the inside of the caverned human mind can be made infinite by means of imagination and art, which by acting upon the stony walls of nature that we have allowed to enclose us reclaims them for humanity. Some Christians might well reserve such labor to God, but Blake again reminds us that God is not in some unknown world elsewhere, but "only Acts and Is, in existing beings or Men" (*CW,* 155).

The fourth Memorable Fancy is a visit to the hell of the conventionally religious—a hell appropriately reached by means of Blake's usual symbol of self-enclosure, the mill. This hell is, like the fallen world that we inhabit, full of threatening objects that we cannot manage without vision: a leviathan striped like a tiger intimidates us "owing to our metaphysics" (as does Blake's famous Tyger), but it does not frighten Blake. Instead, he shows the conventionally religious the hell that they already inhabit in their life in this world:

Soon we saw seven houses of brick; one we enter'd; in it were a number of monkeys, baboons, & all of that species, chain'd by the middle, grinning and snatching at one another, but withheld by the shortness of their chains: however, I saw that they sometimes grew numerous, and then the weak were caught by the strong, and with a grinning aspect, first coupled with, & then devour'd, by plucking off first one limb and then another, till the body was left a helpless trunk; this, after grinning & kissing it with seeming fondness, they devour'd too; and here & there I saw one savourily picking the flesh off of his own tail; as the stench terribly annoy'd us both, we went into the mill, & I in my hand brought the skeleton of a body, which in the mill was Aristotle's Analytics. (*CW,* 157)

The subhuman nature of the inhabitants and their cannibalism remind us what the solipsistic, rational, and analytic mind does to us at every moment of our lives.

Breaking the Restraining Nets

The final Memorable Fancy is Blake's defense of the Jesus of impulse. In words that D. H. Lawrence would echo, Blake calls for a recognition of God's presence in the individual man: "The worship of God is: Honouring his gifts in other men, each according to his genius, and loving the greatest men best: those who envy or calumniate great men hate God; for there is no other God" (*CW*, 158). Although Lawrence would not agree, Blake holds that the mode of God's participation in us is Jesus, the human imagination. As Blake says in his annotations to Berkeley, "man is all Imagination. God is Man & exists in us & we in him (*CW*, 775).

Jesus would hardly have come, therefore, to accuse us of sin; He came to unite us to Him by restoring us to the imagination. Again the annotations to Berkeley may be cited: "The Whole Bible is fill'd with Imagination & Visions from End to End & not with Moral Virtues; that is the business of Plato & the Greeks & all Warriors. The Moral Virtues are continual Accusers of Sin & promote Eternal Wars & Dominency over others" (*CW*, 774). Since "Jesus is the greatest man," He therefore "acted from impulse, not from rules." Systems of moral virtue produce warfare and political tyranny: "One Law for the Lion & Ox is Oppression." We must recognize the energetic Jesus within our own impulses and allow Him to restore us to what we potentially are.

To make sure that the special significance of the outbreak of the French Revolution, as a representation of the growth in vision to which Blake would lead us, is not lost, he appends a "Song of Liberty" to *The Marriage of Heaven and Hell*. Nature itself is shaken by the freeing acts in France ("the Eternal Female groan'd"). Political change is seen as now possible in England ("Albion"), in America, in Spain, and in Rome. The revolutionary energies of Orc ("the new born fire") are released, and Urizen's ("the starry king") attempts to subdue him to "the hand of jealousy" seem ineffective. The hope held out by Blake is for an end not only to political oppression but to the alienation from our full human potential that we have suffered: "Look up! look up! O citizen of London, enlarge thy countenance! O Jew, leave counting gold! return to thy oil and wine. O African! black African! (go, winged thought, widen his forehead)" (*CW,* 159).

The body, which is not distinct from the soul, finds more human proportions despite Urizen's attempts at resistance. Urizen cannot stop this human liberation from an alienated state by opposing it with his system of moral virtues because the energetic Orc "stamps the stony law to dust." No longer, says the chorus, are we to "lay the bound or build the roof" of conventional morality: "For every thing that lives is Holy" (*CW,* 160). To Blake, the accusation of sin is Satan's function. Life is from the imagination, which is divine; nothing imaginative can be sinful, despite the protests of "the Priests of the Raven of dawn."

The Marriage of Heaven and Hell in its recommendation of energy, imagination, and impulse is a fine sourcebook for Blake's thought. One can turn to it for Blake's clear and witty warnings against the denial of energy and for his assertion that firm persuasion is truth, and one can also find in it Blake's clear statement of Milton's limitations and those of Swedenborg. It is perhaps not so major a creation for Blake the poet, however, as are his mythic works in that its insight into the mind is not earned through our participation in mental processes transformed into events like those in *The Book of Urizen.* As a critique of Swedenborg's limitations, the form and the content of *The Marriage* bear too many signs of an occasional work that depends on a parody of the opponent's methods to make debater's points. But this work was at least the necessary refusal on Blake's part to be enslaved by another man's system, even when that man is another great visionary. Its own energy is at any rate full proof of the presence in Blake of the aspect of our humanity that the work would restore to us.

Chapter Five
The French Revolution and *America*

Blake's *French Revolution,* which exists only in a publisher's proof sheet dated 1791, is prefaced with an advertisement that announces that "the remaining Books of this Poem are finished, and will be published in their Order." All that survives is "Book the First," but it is quite possible that *The French Revolution* was indeed finished by Blake as a poem in seven books. Joseph Johnson, who would have been the publisher, apparently lost his nerve when it came to the actual publication of a poem so strongly in favor of the revolution in France—as he had lost his nerve in the case of Thomas Paine's book *The Rights of Man*—but Johnson was an unusually scrupulous publisher who would not be likely to misrepresent the work he meant to offer to the public.

History Made Myth

The French Revolution, like the later work *America* (1793), is remarkable among Blake's poems for presenting a landscape halfway between history and myth. Events of the revolutionary period in France are presented in a recognizable form, but their significance is revealed through apocalyptic imagery and through the actual appearance in the poem, in a dream, of Urizen. Many other poems by Blake have historical meanings, perhaps all do[1]; but the historical events are usually fully translated into mythic ones. In "The Mental Traveller," for instance, political revolution and reaction are seen in terms of contentions between a tormented Orc figure and an old woman who represents nature. In *The French Revolution,* we seem to see the very *process* by which the visionary eye sees through history to the reality beyond it.

The work as we have it is a presentation of the fears of the nobility on the eve of the revolution in France. Lafayette (called "Fayette" by Blake), a leader of the Commons, awaits the charge to lead the army from Paris. The nobles feel, correctly, that the removal of the army will allow a popular uprising. Most of the poem deals with the responses in the debate of the nobility to the mood of prerevolutionary France—although not all of them fear the "fire" of revolt. At the end of the work as it exists, the

Commons recommends that Lafayette proceed to remove the troops; the fears of the nobility seem confirmed, at least in Blake's visionary treatment of the event.

The debate of the nobility is often reminiscent of the one that had ensued in England after the Reverend Richard Price had preached his sermon welcoming the French Revolution. There followed not only the famous reply by Burke in favor of the old order but also numerous replies to Burke that included such notable works as Paine's *Rights of Man* and Godwin's *Political Justice*. Those who favored the Revolution, especially in the Unitarian circles that included Dr. Price, Joseph Priestley, and Blake's almost-publisher Joseph Johnson, often saw it as comprised of events that fitted the pattern of the last things set forth in the Book of Revelations.[2] Blake, too, sees the events as a prelude to apocalypse; but he regards them, characteristically, as the freeing of restrictions on our behavior and perception that starts our return to Eternity. Indeed, he sees the events so totally in the visionary manner that we realize that specific political events, although there are some here, take a definite second place in Blake's mind. Political events for Blake "occur" only as a manifestation of mental events—a manner of looking at revolution that seems well justified in at least so "intellectual" a revolution as that in France.

All revolutions are, for Blake, directed against Urizen, the jealous lawgiver and lover of order, and they are an effort to end the alienation of the contending human faculties symbolized by Blake's mythic figures. Thus Louis XVI appears at the outset of Blake's *French Revolution* in a state of disorganization; from the perspective of Eternity, he is "Sick," "wreath'd in dim / And appalling mist," "cold." His attempt to keep the "mountains" of a Urizenic perspective fixed is, however, now failing: the mountains, the rocky world of our perception, seek to be the "mild flourishing mountains" of Eternity again rather than "the old mountains of France, like aged men." The old order in France is, of course, the result of the vision of "aged men," of Urizenic lawgiving and narrowness. When the king descends to visit his nobles, he joins a den of solipsistic Urizens:

> Forty men, each conversing with woes in the infinite shadows of his soul,
> Like our ancient fathers in regions of twilight, walk, gathering round the King. (*CW*, 134)

The councillors themselves form an enclosure that keeps the king blind to the morning that the rest of France now sees dawning.

From the king, who is, in fact, "imprisoned" by his nobles, we move to the governor of the Bastille, who also wears mental chains:

> in his soul stood the purple plague,
> Tugging his iron manacles, and piercing through the seven towers dark and sickly,
> Panting over the prisoners like a wolf gorg'd. (*CW*, 135)

The prisoners watched over by the governor are the unwilling victims of the perceptual and physical tyranny of the old order. A man with the prophetic and Orc-like "serpent coil'd round in his heart" lives in chains for espousing liberty. Similarly, in "the Den named Religion," a woman who would advocate the forgiveness of sins and consequently denounce the moral categories of a Urizen ("she refus'd to be whore to the minister") is punished with the Law in the form of the seven deadly sins ("The seven diseases of earth"). And a man who "rais'd a pulpit / And taught wonders to darken'd souls" has the most complete punishment of all:

> In the tower nam'd Order, an old man, whose white beard cover'd the stone floor like weeds
> On margin of the sea, shrivel'd up by heat of day and cold of night; his den was short
> And narrow as a grave dug for a child. (*CW*, 135–36)

He has been turned into a Urizen, the perfected ideal of the old order. Another who "pined / For liberty" has been given the Newtonian universe on which the natural religionists meditate:

> his reason decay'd, and the world of attraction in his bosom
> Center'd and the rushing of chaos overwhelm'd his dark soul.
> (*CW*, 136)

The Bastille might indeed be taken to represent the universe, moral and "physical," that Urizen brought into being.

The Debate over "mind-forged manacles"

After all the images of darkness and restriction that we have found
in the description of the Bastille, the imagery based on light and
new birth that surrounds the meeting of the Commons is all the more
welcome:

> a light walks round the dark towers:
> For the Commons convene in the Hall of the Nation, like spirits
> of fire in the beautiful
> Porches of the Sun, to plant beauty in the desart craving abyss,
> they gleam
> On the anxious city; all children new-born first behold them;
> tears are fled.
> And they nestle in earth-breathing bosoms. So the city of Paris,
> their wives and children,
> Look up to the morning Senate, and visions of sorrow leave pen-
> sive streets. (*CW,* 136)

Among the nobles, however, there are only "jealousies," "terrors," and
"gloom." They remain "lock'd up as with strong bands of iron, each
strong limb bound down as with marble / In flames of red wrath burning." As yet, no one instructs them in the uses of fire.

The king again expresses his fears, and the Duke of Burgundy rises to
confirm them. Because the duke will act to check the possibility of new
birth, his speech threatens child sacrifice. "Around him croud, weeping
in his burning robe, / A bright cloud of infant souls; his words fall like
purple autumn on the sheaves," as the duke asks:

> Shall this marble-built heaven become a clay cottage, this earth
> an oak stool, and these mowers
> From the Atlantic mountains mow down all this great starry har-
> vest of six thousand years?
> And shall Necker, the hind of Geneva, stretch out his crook'd
> sickle o'er fertile France
> Till our purple and crimson is faded to russet, and the kingdoms
> of earth bound in sheaves,

And the ancient forests of chivalry hewn, and the joys of combat
burnt for fuel;
Till the power and dominion is rent from the pole, sword and
scepter from sun and moon,
The law and gospel from fire and air, and eternal reason and
science
From the deep and the solid, and man lay his faded head down on
the rock
Of eternity, where the eternal lion and eagle remain to devour?
(*CW,* 138)

Rather than the human scale of "a clay cottage" and an "oak stool,"
Burgundy (like Louis) demands the stony world of Urizen ("marble-built
heaven"). To Blake, "forests" are signs of Urizenic delusion, and he
would say that there can be "joys of combat" only when wars are entirely mental; but Burgundy joins Edmund Burke in bemoaning the end of
an age of chivalry.[3] And, since all error is one in Blake's thought,
Burgundy also defends natural religion—that confused state of mind in
which one seeks "the law and gospel" in the elements and thinks that
science has something to do with "the deep and the solid" rather than
the imaginative.

With a Burgundy to support his worst tendencies, Louis allows "dark
mists" to "roll round" him "and blot the writing of God / Written" within his "bosom." Necker, who would indeed sympathize with the
Commons as Burgundy fears, is driven out of the court; and the
Archbishop of Paris rises to complete the consolidation of error: "the
Archbishop of Paris arose / In the rushing of scales and hissing of flames
and / rolling of sulphurous smoke" (*CW,* 139–40). Not only are his fires
entirely perverted into infernal flames, but he is well on his way to
becoming a member of that snake pit that is the final state of the forces
of evil in Milton's *Paradise Lost.*

Of course, the archbishop speaks of visions of Urizen:

a cold hand passed over my limbs, and behold
An aged form, white as snow, hov'ring in mist, weeping in the
uncertain light.
Dim the form almost faded, tears fell down the shady cheeks.
(*CW,* 140)

Urizen sees in the coming of the revolution the danger that humans will "forget" his "holy law." He fears the end of the alliance of church and state in what is to him a necessary tyranny:

> Nobles and Clergy shall fail from before me, and my cloud and
> vision be no more;
> The mitre become black, the crown vanish, and the scepter and
> ivory staff
> Of the ruler wither among bones of death. (*CW,* 140)

He fears the end of forms and hierarchies:

> They shall drop at the plow and faint at the harrow, unredeem'd,
> unconfess'd, unpardon'd;
> The priest rot in his surplice by the lawless lover, the holy beside
> the accursed,
> The King, frowning in purple, beside the grey plowman, and
> their worms embrace together. (*CW,* 140–41)

Urizen's fears are quite justified; for, to Blake, revolution does mean an end to moral categories and to privilege of all sorts. As would Marx, Blake foresees a postrevolutionary world in which the distinctions originating in the division of labor—between "priest" and "plowman," for instance—have no meaning. The deeply ingrained physical disgust that the ruling class feels for the lower orders is effectively conveyed in Urizen's squeamishness over worms mingling together in flesh of classes not felt to be of the same species. The effect of Urizen's speech on the nobles is, understandably, to so fix them in reaction that the weeping infants surrounding them are replaced by the nobles' own deformed spawn: "monsters of worlds unknown / Swam round them watching to be delivered." The Archbishop of Paris is himself now totally a snake, Blake's usual image for the evils of priestcraft: he is unable to rise to his feet and "instead of words harsh hissings / Shook the chamber."

Next, the defenders of the revolution and of imagination speak. The first, the Duke of Orleans, undertakes the task of trying to bring the nobles to an understanding of their own human possibility: "O princes of fire, whose flames are for growth, not consuming, / Fear not dreams, fear not visions, nor be you dismay'd with sorrows which flee at the morning!" (*CW,* 142). An individual's fire—the energy and imagination that one possesses—is not to be feared and repressed: "Fire delights in its form." One person cannot make laws to govern another's flames:

> Go, thou cold recluse, into the fires
> Of another's high flaming rich bosom, and return, unconsum'd, and write laws.
> If thou canst not do this, doubt thy theories; learn to consider all men as thy equals,
> Thy brethren, and not as thy foot or thy hand, unless thou first fearest to hurt them. (*CW,* 142–43)

All are equal because all possess the divine imagination, and any political or theological system that denies this equality is tyrannous.

The Abbé de Sieyès arrives from the Commons to complete the education of the nobles by means of a history of the origins of the Urizenic universe and a forecast of its fate:

> When the heavens were seal'd with a stone, and the terrible sun clos'd in an orb, and the moon
> Rent from the nations, and each star appointed for watchers of night,
> The millions of spirits immortal were bound in the ruins of sulphur heaven
> To wander enslav'd; black, deprest in dark ignorance, kept in awe with the whip
> To worship terrors, bred from the blood of revenge and breath of desire
> In bestial forms, or more terrible men; till the dawn of our peaceful morning,
> Till dawn, till morning, till the breaking of clouds, and swelling of winds, and the universal voice;
> Till man raise his darken'd limbs out of the caves of night; his eyes and his heart
> Expand: where is Space? where, O Sun, is thy dwelling? where thy tent, O faint slumbrous Moon? (*CW,* 143–44)

What the nobles fear as political revolution is in fact, for all people, a movement away from closed perception and alienation from their real selves. A world of peace, love, and art is promised:

> the saw, and the hammer, the chisel, the pencil, the pen, and the instruments
> Of heavenly song sound in the wilds once forbidden, to teach the laborious plowman
> And shepherd, deliver'd from clouds of war, from pestilence, from nightfear, from murder,
> From falling, from stifling, from hunger, from cold, from slander, discontent and sloth,
> That walk in beasts and birds of night, driven back by the sandy desart
> Like pestilent fogs round cities of men; and the happy earth sing in its course,
> The mild peaceable nations be opened to heav'n, and men walk with their fathers in bliss. (CW, 144–45)

All labor will then be art; whatever frightens us in nature (such as Blake's Tyger, the best-known of the "beasts . . . of the night" that he depicts) will be tamed; all will be "open'd to heav'n" to end restriction, enclosure, secrecy, and metaphysics; everyone will fulfill humanity's original, prelapsarian potential (and thus "walk with their fathers in bliss"). But the nobles cannot understand these words as anything but a threat.

The Political Road to Apocalypse

When the Commons orders Lafayette to lead the army away, the visionary meaning of his obedience to their command is made evident by Blake:

> Like a flame of fire he stood before dark ranks, and before expecting captains:
> On pestilent vapours around him flow frequent spectres of religious men, weeping
> In winds, driven out of the abbeys, their naked souls shiver in keen open air;

> Driven out by the fiery cloud of Voltaire, and thunderous rocks of
> Rousseau,
> They dash like foam against the ridges of the army, uttering a
> faint feeble cry. (*CW*, 146)

Voltaire and Rousseau, thinkers whose views Blake fiercely opposed, are
nonetheless of value to the revolution because of their opposition to
institutionalized religion—to priestcraft and state religion. The serpent-
nobility surround the king, who seems in any case near death ("Pale and
cold . . . his pulses / Suspended"):

> The cold newt
> And snake and damp toad on the kingly foot crawl, or croak on
> the awful knee,
> Shedding their slime; in folds of the robe the crown'd adder
> builds and hisses
> From stony brows; shaken the forests of France, sick the kings of
> the nations,
> And the bottoms of the world were open'd, and the graves of
> archangels unseal'd:
> The enormous dead lift up their pale fires and look over the rocky
> cliffs. (*CW*, 147–48)

The forests of error, the stony world itself, await the apocalypse.
Repressed energy and vision ("The enormous dead") are at last free to
play their role in ending human alienation. Much more of the story
remains to be told, but the debaters of book 1 have moved us to the
margins of Eternity, as Blake's contending forces so often do. In these
heartening years, the growth in mental powers to which Blake invites us
was in France producing substantive political events. *The French
Revolution,* with its willingness to see history both with and through the
eye, was the happy outcome of this dynamic process.

An American Analogue

Although the revolution in nearby France would continue to influence
English civilization and politics for years to come, the revolutionary period in Western history had of course opened with the American

Revolution. Having written *The French Revolution,* Blake turned to the earlier American events and interpreted them as similarly apocalyptic signs. *America* (1793) needs less commentary than *The French Revolution* because it is a less difficult work.

An American reader may be gratified to find George Washington, Benjamin Franklin, Tom Paine, John Hancock, and other American heroes allied with a fiery adolescent Orc in a rebellion that simultaneously rejects delusive Nature and George III. The imagery is that of the Resurrection ("The grave is burst, the spices shed, the linen wrapped up") because the events in America are a first step on the way to a reborn Divine Humanity that is free of restrictive moral codes and life-denying institutions:

> The doors of marriage are open, and the Priests in rustling scales
> Rush into reptile coverts, hiding from the fires of Orc,
> That play around the golden roofs in wreaths of fierce desire,
> Leaving the females naked and glowing with the lusts of youth.
> For the female spirits of the dead, pining in bonds of religion,
> Run from their fetters reddening, & in long drawn arches sitting,
> They feel the nerves of youth renew, and desires of ancient times
> Over their pale limbs, as a vine when the tender grape appears.
> (*CW,* 202)

Thus, in *America,* as in *The French Revolution,* Blake demonstrates that any step taken in behalf of freedom is a step toward the perfect liberty of Eternity. In both works he retains recognizable historical events and persons, while supplying their visionary meanings. In these works Blake shows how he read the events of his time and encourages speculation about how he would read the events of subsequent times: imagination and energy have not always defeated the forces of repression as they did in the French and American Revolutions.

Chapter Six

Visions of the Daughters of Albion

William Blake offered his vigorous support to the cause of the emancipation of women when he wrote *Visions of the Daughters of Albion* (1793). The restrictions placed on women are the result of jealousy, a quality exemplified in Urizen because jealousy demands an environment in which all will submit to control and be subject to "one law." Since the emotion of jealousy exists in the "natural heart" that Urizen has given us in forcing us to perceive a separate and determining physical world, Blake's epigraph for the *Visions* is "The Eye sees more than the [natural] Heart knows." Seeing through the eye, Blake will reveal the errors about society, nature, and human identity that find ideological support through the nets of jealousy, and he will begin to construct an oppositional outlook.

The heroine of *Visions of the Daughters of Albion* is Oothoon, who is "the soft soul of America" and who is, therefore, the representative of liberty, as is Jerusalem. Her plight, her unsatisfied aspiration for liberty, is the plight of all the women of England, and this poem is a visionary insight into their condition. But in another sense we are all, male and female, the "daughters of Albion" who await the restoration of our liberty. ("Jerusalem is named liberty / Among the sons of Albion" [*CW*, 649].) To keep the universality of Oothoon's plight before us, Blake throughout calls upon all "daughters of Albion" to function as a chorus: "Enslav'd, the daughters of Albion weep: a trembling lamentation / Upon their mountains; in their valleys, sighs towards America" (*CW*, 189); "The Daughters of Albion hear her woes, & eccho back her sighs" (*CW*, 190). The device effectively reminds us that we must seek for a solution to Oothoon's dilemma by exploring our own lives and minds.

The events of the poem are few. Oothoon had hesitated in her "virgin fears" to undertake a physical relationship with Theotormon, whom she loves. But, told by the Marygold that "the soul of sweet delight / Can never pass away," she learns that the loss of virginity is not—despite the attitudes of her culture—a change in identity. ("Every Harlot was a Virgin once," Blake writes elsewhere. "Nor can'st thou ever change Kate into Nan" [*CW*, 771].) But, before she can find Theotormon, presumably simply to marry him, she is attacked by an "accuser of sin" who might be Urizen or Satan but who is named Bromion. Bromion brands her a "harlot" for her attitudes, and Theotormon then fears her too. Commentators on this poem have generally missed the point that Bromion's "rape" of Oothoon is precisely his labeling her with a word taken from the moral code that Blake follows Jesus in rejecting. Bromion's forcing of human impulse into a moral category is an act of violence against a human being. As a result, Bromion, an accuser of sin, and Oothoon, a representative of liberty, are tied back to back in a cave by the "jealous" Theotormon (whose name probably means "God-tormented," one tortured by holding the mistaken vision of God the lawgiver rather than of the Jesus who preaches "mutual forgiveness of sins").

A debate follows among these three about the issues of freedom and restraint; but no resolution occurs because nothing has yet changed for the daughters of Albion. Nonetheless, the debate tells us much about the origins of some of our most fundamental attitudes. Bromion's labeling of Oothoon as a harlot is a Urizenic assertion of control over her that is the same act of mind that allows one human being to own another in slavery:

Bromion spoke: "Behold this harlot here on Bromion's bed,
And let the jealous dolphins sport around the lovely maid!
Thy soft American plains are mine, and mine thy north & south:
Stampt with my signet are the swarthy children of the sun;
They are obedient, they resist not, they obey the scourge;
Their daughters worship terrors and obey the violent." (*CW*, 190)

In fact, this sort of assertion of personal control over someone or something, this "jealousy," must be recognized as the origin of private property. Blake was like Marx in wanting "All Things Common" (*CW*, 777).

If the label "harlot" is a challenge to Theotormon's male pride—one that forces him to perform his jealous act of binding Oothoon to Bromion, her accuser—then Theotormon, too, is the victim of attitudes that have perpetuated social evils: "beneath him sound like waves on a desart shore / The voice of slaves beneath the sun, and children bought with money, / That shiver in religious caves" (*CW*, 190).

Social evils such as slavery, corrupt institutions, poverty, and war are all the result of our participation in the jealous and commodifying vision of Urizen: could our perspective be changed, all "external" to us would change. Oothoon alone can see clearly because she is "the soft soul of America," and she has picked the Marygold. "Arise, my Theotormon," she pleads, "I am pure"; and she offers an account of that fundamental error in perception that has created all our misery:

They told me that the night & day were all that I could see;
They told me that I had five senses to inclose me up,
And they inclos'd my infinite brain into a narrow circle,
And sunk my heart into the Abyss, a red, round globe, hot burning,
Till all from life I was obliterated and erased. (*CW,* 191)

She begs us to remember that impulse would have a major role to play if we were to heed it: "ask . . . the wing'd eagle why he loves the sun; / And then tell me the thoughts of man, that have been hid of old." But no one understands what she is saying.

Theotormon is so thoroughly Urizenic in his attitudes that any appeal based on the value of impulse is meaningless to him ("what is the night or day to one o'erflow'd with woe?"). Instead, he wants what jealousy always wants—a rigid, fixed world:

Tell me what is a thought, & of what *substance* is it made?
Tell me what is a joy, & *in what gardens* do joys grow?
And *in what rivers* swim the sorrows? and *upon what mountains*
Wave shadows of discontent? and *in what houses* dwell the wretched,
Drunken with woe forgotten, and shut up from cold despair? (*CW,*
191–92; italics added)

Theotormon's demand that thoughts be things ("substance") and have physical location ("in what gardens . . . in what rivers . . . upon what mountains . . . in what houses") exactly repeats the error in perception that creates our physical world. Bromion's condition is even more diseased; for, not contented with one physical world to possess in jealous vision, he wants more such worlds. He seeks them even "in the infinite microscope," an activity absurd to Blake, who knows that such investigators bring their own fallen vision to what is called "scientific observation" and see, therefore, only their own limitations in what they think they observe. As happened with Urizen, Bromion's mistaken sense that fixity can exist and is desirable produces not just the sort of physical world he inhabits but the kind of moral world he would try to force on humankind: "And is there not one law for both the lion and the ox? / And is there not eternal fire and eternal chains / To bind the phantoms of existence from eternal life?" (*CW*, 192). Not sharing Oothoon's new understanding of the possibilities for cleansing the gates of perception, Bromion and Theotormon can never understand her arguments for a new view of morality.

Oothoon rightly attacks Urizen, who in Blake's myth is largely responsible for all that we endure:

O Urizen! Creator of men! mistaken Demon of heaven!
Thy joys are tears, thy labour vain to form men to thine image.
How can one joy absorb another? are not different joys
Holy, eternal, infinite? And each joy is a Love. (*CW*, 192)

She talks about the treatment of women in our civilization ("bound / In spells of law to one she loathes") and points to female and male masturbation as "the places of religion, the rewards of continence, / The self enjoyings of self denial":

The virgin
That pines for man shall awaken her womb to enormous joys
In the secret shadows of her chamber: the youth shut up from
The lustful joy shall forget to generate & create an amorous image
In the shadows of his curtains and in the folds of his silent pillow. (*CW*, 194)

Masturbation is even now a subject that is rarely mentioned in poetry and that has become the subject of controversy when proposed as an issue in public discourse; but it is a fact of life appropriately addressed in Oothoon's pleas. Not only is masturbation the usual outcome of the sexual denial that both Blake and Oothoon oppose, but it is the physical manifestation of a society that denies relationship and commodifies the opposite sex, thereby creating the tormenting object and the private, secretive subject that Blake and Marx saw to be the definitive feature of bourgeois philosophy. Herself abhorring all secrecy, Oothoon welcomes openness and sunshine:

Open to joy and to delight where ever beauty appears;
If in the morning sun I find it, there my eyes are fix'd
In happy copulation; if in evening mild, wearied with work,
Sit on a bank and draw the pleasures of this free born joy.

. . . .

I cry: Love! Love! Love! happy happy Love!—free as the mountain
wind!"

. . . .

Arise, and drink your bliss, for every thing that lives is holy!" (*CW*,
194–95)

Theotormon, who understands none of her declaration, turns from the
possibility of sunshine that Oothoon holds out and converses "with shadows dire."

Oothoon even suggests a kind of shock treatment to let Theotormon
see that jealousy is not a necessary part of human makeup:

silken nets and traps of adamant will Oothoon spread,
And catch for thee girls of mild silver, or of furious gold.
I'll lie beside thee on a bank & view their wanton play
In lovely copulation, bliss on bliss, with Theotormon:
Red as the rosy morning, lustful as the first born beam,
Oothoon shall view his dear delight, nor e'er with jealous cloud
Come in the heaven of generous love, nor selfish blightings bring. (*CW*,
194–95)

It is perhaps just as well that Theotormon is not given a chance to reply
to this suggestion. Oothoon's world and perception are perhaps shock-
ingly open, but Theotormon's are tragically closed. While such "jealousy" exists, bringing with it the evils of slavery and private property,
the women of England cannot be free—and men and women alike will
inhabit this world of "substance" and "one law."

Chapter Seven

Songs of Innocence and of Experience

Blake had published the *Songs of Innocence* (1789) and the *Songs of Experience* (c. 1793) separately before their appearance together in 1794; but only when he linked those works with the new title *Songs of Innocence and of Experience* (1794) did he complete the execution of the complex and masterful work that contains his most widely read poetry. Much of the greatness of the work for any reader, and at any level that one might read it, arises from the juxtaposition of two modes of vision—Innocence and Experience. Blake's subtitle tells us that these modes of vision deserve to be respected as "contraries"; therefore, they are both "Good" (*CW*, 91), and both are necessary to "progression" (*CW*, 149) toward the full, unalienated Divine Humanity that was forfeited in the revolt of Urizen.

Attempts by critics to make the *Songs of Innocence* ironic, to suggest that Blake undercuts or even mocks the perspective and language of Innocence, are based on an inadequate grasp of Blake's thought. The state of Innocence, possessed by each of us in childhood or in fantasy, is the proof that we possess the powerful, creative, and divine imagination. Experience is, on the other hand, the analytic state of mind that finds the limits of the world that our fallen perception gives us. Both states are "necessary to Human existence" (*CW*, 149), Blake would say; and we must remember that in Blake's thought authentic "Human existence" becomes possible only when we participate in the Divine Humanity in Eternity.

Innocence: Pastoralism as Vision

In the *Songs of Innocence,* pastoralism is the controlling convention, but Blake attains far more with his use of pastoralism than the simplification of relationships that the convention usually achieves. For Blake, the shepherd-sheep relationship and the special world inhabited by shepherd and sheep become the way of representing the characteristic mode of perception in the state of Innocence. Poems such as "The Lamb," "The Shepherd," "The Little Boy Lost/The Little Boy Found," "A Dream,"

"Nurse's Song," "A Cradle Song," and "On Another's Sorrow" project the innocent's ability to recast the world imaginatively into one where we can not only be at home but also be cared for by a loving shepherd. It is pointless to object that such a world does not exist in what seems to be the world of common sense and "experience": such an objection would be raised by a Bacon or by a similar advocate of ratio perception. Stanley Gardner has, moreover, demonstrated that at the time that these songs were written Blake shared the hope that childhood innocence was being protected and nurtured in the reformed charity school in the Parish of St. James; Blake lived near the school and his father had supplied its haberdashery, so he would have known of its successes (Gardner 1986).

The finest poems of the *Songs of Innocence* are those in which there is some admission of the hardships actually faced by the innocents of the world under harsher circumstances than those in the parish school; but in these poems the innocent view can be seen as easily transcending adversity. "The Chimney Sweeper" is such a poem:

When my mother died I was very young,
And my Father sold me while yet my tongue
Could scarcely cry "'weep! 'weep! 'weep! 'weep!"
So your chimneys I sweep, & in soot I sleep.

There's little Tom Dacre, who cried when his head,
That curl'd like a lamb's back, was shav'd: so I said
Hush, Tom! never mind it, for when your head's bare
You know that the soot cannot spoil your white hair."

And so he was quiet, & that very night
As Tom was a-sleeping, he had such a sight!
That thousands of sweepers, Dick, Joe, Ned, & Jack,
Were all of them lock'd up in coffins of black.

And by came an Angel who had a bright key,
And he open'd the coffins & set them all free;
Then down a green plain leaping, laughing, they run,
And wash in a river, and shine in the Sun.

Then naked & white, all their bags left behind,
They rise upon clouds and sport in the wind;
And the Angel told Tom, if he'd be a good boy,
He'd have God for his father, & never want joy.

And so Tom awoke; and we rose in the dark,
And got with our bags & our brushes to work.
Tho' the morning was cold, Tom was happy & warm;
So if all do their duty they need not fear harm. (*CW,* 117–18)

We know that the conditions faced by chimney sweepers in the eighteenth century could not have been more inhuman. Tiny, half-starved children died of suffocation or of skin cancer as a result of the employment into which they were indeed "sold." Yet the innocent vision of this poem converts that harsh world into a world of shepherds and sheep: Tom Dacre[1] had white hair as do lambs, and it "curl'd like a lamb's back." When our world cannot support the pastoral vision, Innocence transfers it to an afterlife where chimney sweepers "will sport like lambs ("down a green plain leaping, laughing they run, / And wash in a river and shine in the sun") and where they will have a loving father who will be their shepherd ("have God for [a] father, & never want joy").

This afterlife of a sentimental theology is based on false, or at least irrelevant, moral platitudes ("if all do their duty they need not fear harm"); but it is still an imaginative vision that, experienced by all at times, is proof of human powers. We easily transcend the world of ratio perception, no matter what the claims of the "real world" seem to be. Thus a poem like "The Chimney Sweeper" relies on neither undercutting nor irony: the ability to envision pastoral relationships, despite the world that we currently occupy, is proof of our divinity.

Another fine example of the indomitable character of innocent vision is "The Little Black Boy," in which the horrors of racism and the slave trade—which Blake joined the leaders of the Evangelical movement in opposing—are not ignored but transcended by the vision of the little black boy. His mother's sentimental theology has taught him that "we shall hear his voice, / Saying: 'Come out from the grove, my love & care, / And round my golden tent like lambs rejoice'" (*CW,* 125). He looks forward to a time "When I from black and he from white cloud free, / . . . round the tent of God like lambs we joy" (*CW,* 125). The shepherd-and-sheep relationship replaces the reality of oppression. "[H]e will then love me," the little black boy says; and the word "then" carries the admission of the current relationship between the races. But even so, the joyful tone is not undercut, and the innocent vision triumphs.

"Holy Thursday" pictures the charity children who are brought into St. Paul's on Ascension Day as "multitudes of lambs" who are tended by beadles with "wands as white as snow." Despite the poverty that the children embody, they bring "radiance"; and "like a mighty wind they raise to heaven the voice of song." With the beadles as shepherds, as "wise guardians," they exist happily within the pastoral world of Innocence. A sight such as is presented in this poem seems to justify the pious conclusion "cherish pity lest you drive an angel from your door." Outside the perspective of Innocence, Blake argues that, since pity simply accepts existing evils, it is not a virtue; for that "contrary" viewpoint, and related insights, one must turn to the *Songs of Experience.*

The Mode of Experience: The Analytic Harrow

Without the perspective of Innocence, says Blake, humans would not be aware of our powers and would remain unable to benefit from what the analysis of the *Songs of Experience* offers us. With the pastoral world of restored relationship and psychological health also kept in mind, "Holy Thursday" in *Experience* voices a revolutionary demand for the full humanity of Eternity:

> Is this a holy thing to see
> In a rich and fruitful land,
> Babes reduc'd to misery,
> Fed with cold and usurous hand?
>
> Is that trembling cry a song?
> Can it be a song of joy?
> And so many children poor?
> It is a land of poverty!
>
> And their sun does never shine,
> And their fields are bleak & bare,
> And their ways are fill'd with thorns:
> It is eternal winter there.

For where-e'er the sun does shine,
And where-e'er the rain does fall,
Babe can never hunger there,
Nor poverty the mind appall. (*CW,* 211–12)

Human life has been cast within an unnatural world, one created by acquiescence to the rift between subject and object promoted by Lockean psychology and the economic system that it sustains. Thus, in the introduction to *Experience,* the Bard (the Poetic Genius or Imagination within us) calls to the earth itself:

O Earth, O Earth, return!
Arise from out the dewy grass;
. . . .
The starry floor,
The wat'ry shore,
Is giv'n thee till the break of day. (*CW,* 210)

The heavens, "floored off" by the stars that we think are fixed in their patterns above us, will be opened again by the divine imagination. All that prevents our reaching upward and pulling down the heavens with our bare hands, as Los does in *The Four Zoas,* is our confused mental state—shared by an entire civilization—that Blake documents mythically in the history of the usurpation of our powers by Urizen. Thus "Earth's Answer" to the Bard:

Prison'd on wat'ry shore,
Starry jealousy does keep my den:
Cold and hoar,
Weeping o'er,
I hear the Father of the ancient men.

Selfish father of men!
Cruel, jealous, selfish fear!
Can delight,
Chain'd in night,
The virgins of youth and morning bear?
. . . .

> Break this heavy chain
> That does freeze my bones around.
> Selfish! vain!
> Eternal bane!
> That free Love with bondage bound. (*CW,* 211)

It is the "jealousy" that requires a fixed universe and rigid moral codes that has made the world of our experience an unnatural desert. Urizen, "cold and hoar," "weeping," has caused us to be "chain'd in night" and divorced from the "delight" of energy and imagination. Quite literally, "free love" would in Blake's view break down the Urizenic universe that is based on law and restraint. Blake simultaneously stresses the philosophic, psychological, and political origins of all the suffering that we seem forced to endure in the world of Experience.

"The Tyger," Blake's best-known poem,[2] is also one of his best accounts of the origins of the limited and terrifying world that we inhabit. "The roaring of lions, the howling of wolves, the raging of the stormy sea, and the destructive sword, are portions of eternity, too great for the eye of man" (*CW,* 151), Blake said in *The Marriage of Heaven and Hell.* The mere fact that tigers exist in this world to threaten us is proof of the inadequacy of the world that we have conceived. Blake brings the Tyger fully to life before us:

> And what shoulder, & what art,
> Could twist the sinews of thy heart?
> And when thy heart began to beat,
> What dread hand? & what dread feet?
>
> What the hammer? what the chain?
> In what furnace was thy brain?
> What the anvil? what dread grasp
> Dare its deadly terrors clasp? (*CW,* 214)

The insistent questioning reproduces the very heartbeat of the Tyger and the blows on the anvil struck by the Tyger's creator who is, of course, the fallen human imagination that is called Los by Blake and that is necessarily the source of everything in the world. "When the stars threw down their spears [their rays]," the creation was completed in the fixing

of "the starry floor." Who then made the Tyger? We did, with our fallen
and limited perception that separates the universe from Eternity and fills
a world with threatening objects.

   In Eternity, the humanized world of life in the Divine Humanity,
tigers will be seen as men with yellow hair. The result of such a rehumanization is what Lyca's parents encounter in "The Little Girl Found"
in *Experience,* when they expect to see a lion:

> They look upon his eyes
> Fill'd with deep surprise,
> And wondering behold
> A Spirit arm'd in gold.
>
> On his head a crown,
> On his shoulders down
> Flow'd his golden hair.
> Gone was all their care. (*CW,* 114)

   When our perception is restored, a human world will surround us
totally. As Blake explains in *Milton,*

These are the Sons of Los, & these the Labourers of the Vintage.
Thou seest the gorgeous clothed Flies that dance & sport in summer
Upon the sunny brooks & meadows: every one the dance
Knows in its intricate mazes of delight artful to weave:
Each one to sound his instruments of music in the dance,
To touch each other & recede, to cross & change & return:

These are the Children of Los; thou seest the Trees on mountains,
The wind blows heavy, loud they thunder thro' the darksom sky,
Uttering prophecies & speaking instructive words to the sons
Of men: These are the Sons of Los: These are the Visions of Eternity,
But we see only as it were the hem of their garments
When with our vegetable eyes we view these wondrous Visions.
(*CW,* 512)

Because our perception accepts the rift between subject and object, we have closed off such worlds of delight. In "The Little Girl Found," Blake presents the restored world that allows us to see the human lion. He has looked forward to such a restoration in "The Little Girl Lost":

> In futurity
> I prophetic see
> That the earth from sleep
> (Grave the sentence deep)
>
> Shall arise and seek
> For her maker meek;
> And the desart wild
> Become a garden mild. (*CW,* 112)

The pair of poems "The Little Girl Lost" and "Little Girl Found" was appropriately moved from its earlier position in *Innocence:* the poems do look forward to Eternity itself rather than offer the comfort of the innocent vision as does, for instance, "The Chimney Sweeper." Lyca's parents find their lost child not in a pastoral world but in the fully human world of Eternity.

The Deserts of Albion

The magnificent poem "London" in *Experience* traces the way in which our philosophic and psychological confusion has been projected into the kind of institutions of which we are willing parts. Blake's repetitions emphasize the rigid patterning that our perception carries out and the rigid confining trap that we have come to inhabit:

> I wander thro' each *charter'd* street,
> Near where the *charter'd* Thames does flow,
> And *mark in every face* I meet
> *Marks of weakness, marks* of woe.
>
> *In every cry of every Man,*
> *In every* Infant's *cry* of fear,

> *In every voice, in every ban,*
> The mind-forg'd manacles I hear. (*CW,* 216; italics added)

London, which Blake's myth says should be Jerusalem, has become
instead the fullest manifestation of a civilization whose life is based on
bad mental habits—on "mind-forg'd manacles." "Prisons are built with
stones of Law, Brothels with bricks of Religion," Blake said in *The
Marriage of Heaven and Hell*; and we see in his "London" how the failures
of the church and state are made evident through the misery that they
cause:

> How the Chimney-sweeper's cry
> Every blackening Church appalls;
> And the hapless Soldier's sigh
> Runs in blood down Palace walls. (*CW,* 216)

The chimney sweeper is blackened by the church that permits children
to be sold into this form of slavery; and thus, to any Christian eye, the
chimney sweeper blackens the church in return. The state is revealed as
the bloody machine of war that it is through Blake's brilliant image of
the sigh that turns to blood once it comes in contact with the palace
wall. And the institution of marriage, because it sets rigid limits on what
is permissible sexual behavior, is seen to have contracted the harlot's disease:

> But most thro' midnight streets I hear
> How the youthful Harlot's curse
> Blasts the new born Infant's tear,
> And blights with plagues the Marriage hearse. (*CW,* 216)

London has become a black, bloody, and diseased desert because of the
mental habits of those who rule it and of those who acquiesce in their
rule.

Into a world like that of "London" we must be born in "Infant
Sorrow." We are restricted from birth:

> Struggling in my father's hands,
> Striving against my swadling bands,

> Bound and weary I thought best
> To sulk upon my mother's breast. (*CW,* 217)

We suffer as in "The Schoolboy" ("How can the bird that is born for joy / Sit in a cage and sing?"); and our sexual passions, our impulses toward an apocalyptic freeing by means of love, are checked as in "The Garden of Love":

> I went to the Garden of Love
> And saw what I never had seen:
> A Chapel was built in the midst,
> Where I used to play on the green.
>
> And the gates of this Chapel were shut,
> And "Thou shalt not" writ over the door;
> So I turn'd to the Garden of Love
> That so many sweet flowers bore;
>
> And I saw it was filled with graves,
> And tomb-stones where flowers should be;
> And Priests in black gowns were walking their rounds,
> And binding with briars my joys & desires. (*CW,* 215)

Quite consistently, Blake's imagery for depicting our condition in *Experience* is based on limitation and on restriction, on binding and on enclosure.

If the love of rigidity and Urizenic "jealousy" of the institutions of its civilization turn Albion—England—into a desert through an external application of the Moral Code, we contribute to the dehumanization of other people and ourselves through our own jealous fear that someone will not adhere to our narrow expectations and sense of propriety. Thus, when the "Pretty Rosetree" (*CW,* 215) fears, without cause, that the speaker of the poem has accepted another "sweet flower," "my Rose turn'd away with jealousy, / And her thorns were my only delight." Self-corrupted and rendering life painful to others, this jealous rose appears again in Blake's "Sick Rose":

O Rose, thou art sick!
The invisible worm
That flies in the night,
In the howling storm,

Has found out thy bed
Of crimson joy:
And his dark secret love
Does thy life destroy. (*CW,* 213)

With his image of the "invisible worm," Blake allows us to see jealousy itself as it goes about its work. As always in Blake, what is "dark" and "secret" is the antithesis of life, and remembering the "tomb-stones where flowers should be" from "The Garden of Love," on this plate we watch jealousy a "life destroy."

"The Chimney Sweeper" in *Experience* now sees through what seems the sentimental escapism of the speaker of "The Chimney Sweeper" in *Innocence:*

because I am happy & dance & sing,
They think they have done me no injury,
And are gone to praise God & his Priest & King,
Who make up a heaven of our misery." (*CW,* 212)

The happiness of the chimney sweepers is, in fact, without foundation, and their hoped-for escape to a better world is a palliative put together by the alliance of church and state that Blake detested. Blake would have agreed with Soame Jenyns, the amateur theologian of the eighteenth century, who wrote, "impossible it must be that a divine and human Government should subsist together in the same Society, for they must immediately clash; and whenever that happens, the least spark of divine authority, if really divine, must infallibly consume all human power, and destroy all Civil Government whatever."[3] Divine government would mean an end to secular government; therefore, any alliance of Priest and king that endures can be seen as having perverted—or killed—whatever was divine in it.

The SICK ROSE

O Rose thou art sick.
The invisible worm,
That flies in the night
In the howling storm:

Has found out thy bed
Of crimson joy:
And his dark secret love
Does thy life destroy.

"The Little Boy Lost" is based on the false hierarchy in love that is often required of us. Blake sees that we must first love the Divine Humanity within ourselves:

> Nought loves another as itself,
> Nor venerates another so,
> Nor is it possible to Thought
> A greater than itself to know. (*CW,* 218)

For the little boy's refusal to "love" according to institutional prescription, he undergoes the usual punishment of the revolutionary figure (Orc) in Blake's work:

> They strip'd him to his little shirt,
> And bound him in an iron chain;
> And burn'd him in a holy place,
> Where many had been burn'd before:
> The weeping parents wept in vain.
> Are such things done on Albion's shore? (*CW,* 218–19)

For Blake, the practice of child sacrifice—whether literal or metaphorical—is the sure sign of a civilization devoted to natural religion. "Are such things done on Albion's shore?" Blake asks. The answer is yes for any land that, virtually by force, turns its children away from what is imaginative and authentic.

Many of the poems in *The Songs of Experience* are written in advocacy of "That free Love" that is presently "with bondage bound." Among these poems, perhaps the best, and certainly the most effectively condensed, is "The Lilly":

> The modest Rose puts forth a thorn,
> The humble Sheep a threatening horn,
> While the Lilly white shall in love delight,
> Nor a thorn, nor a threat, stain her beauty bright. (*CW,* 215)

The rose's practice of modesty and the sheep's habit of humility disfigure them with "thorn" and "horn." The lily remains unstained because of its spontaneous participation in the "delight" of love. For Blake, modesty and humility are the virtues of those who prefer restraint and secrecy. He denies that Jesus was humble,[4] and he assigns "mild humility" to the "sneaking serpent" of the conventionally religious.[5]

Transcending the Limits of Mortality

"The Fly," a poem whose meaning has been widely debated, makes the fundamentally Blakean assertion that reality is created through the blending of subject and object in human experience. We can have knowledge, Blake believes, only of that in which the human mind participates, but the activity of that mind is part of Divine Humanity, the unalienated condition that Blake calls Eternity[6]:

> thought is life
> And strength & breath,
> And the want
> Of thought is death. (*CW*, 213)

If this assertion is true, we need not fear death:

> Then am I
> A happy fly,
> If I live
> Or if I die. (*CW*, 213)

In the very act of perceiving and accepting our physical bodies, we acquiesce in the efforts of our civilization and economy to limit and commodify us; but, as "The Fly" asserts, the condition in which one is entirely an object without subjectivity has no human meaning. Similarly, Blake tells us in "To Tirzah" that we need not feel tied to anything that is mortal:

> Whate'er is Born of Mortal Birth
> Must be consumed with the Earth
> To rise from Generation free:
> Then what have I to do with thee?

"Nature" has limited and warped us:

> Thou, Mother of my Mortal part,
> With cruelty didst mould my Heart,
> And with false self-deceiving tears
> Didst bind my Nostrils, Eyes, & Ears:
>
> Didst close my Tongue in senseless clay,
> And me to Mortal Life betray.

But we are as superior to nature as to mortality: "The Death of Jesus set me free: / Then what have I to do with thee?" (*CW,* 220).

In "The Fly" and "To Tirzah," we receive Blake's assurance that the limited and painful understanding of human life that most people have had at least since the Renaissance is to be transcended by resumption of unalienated humanity. The "world of Imagination is Infinite & Eternal, whereas the world of Generation, or Vegetation, is Finite & Temporal" (*CW,* 605).

The Natural Cycle in *The Book of Thel*

It is appropriate to discuss *The Book of Thel* as a footnote to *The Songs of Innocence and of Experience* because *Thel*'s theme is the passage from Innocence into Experience that we all must undergo. Blake has Enion, one of his mythic characters, lament:

> What is the price of Experience? do men buy it for a song?
> Or wisdom for a dance in the street? No, it is bought with the price
> Of all that a man hath. (*CW,* 290)

The same idea forms the basis of the headnote to *The Book of Thel*:

> Does the Eagle know what is in the pit?
> Or wilt thou go ask the Mole?
> Can Wisdom be put in a silver rod?
> Or love in a golden bowl? (*CW,* 127)

The point is simply that wisdom is painfully won by humankind—won by passage through and finally revolt against the inhuman acts and restrictions Blake depicts in the *Songs of Experience*. We have neither "silver rod" nor "golden bowl" but must endure the pains of the senses—and a life of a body that the philosophy and economics of our age endeavor to make both object and commodity—before winning our way back to Eternity.

Thel is, therefore, a maiden who recognizes, quite rightly, that although lily, cloud, worm, and clod of clay are satisfied by their roles in nature, humanity is not. The brevity and apparent uselessness of Thel's life moves her to ask for some significant role for herself. But all that she is offered, all that humans within nature are ever offered, is the opportunity to be food for worms. Her restlessness—her demand for something better—has already caused her to be unsuited for life in the pastoral world of Innocence which, in our lives as fallen humanity, must end with the recognition that the world into which we are born will neither sustain our vision nor answer our demands for personal happiness.

Thel is forced to accept the life of the senses in the physical body:

She saw the couches of the dead, & where the fibrous roots
Of every heart on earth infixes deep its restless twists:
A land of sorrows & of tears where never smile was seen. (*CW,* 130)

The natural heart is tied to the natural world to be only a source of torment to us: it is the punishment usually meted out to Orc, who, although he represents our impulse to break down limits, is tied to the physical world in restraint. The "grave" Thel visits is, therefore, her own body:

waiting oft beside a dewy grave
She stood in silence, list'ning to the voices of the ground,
Till to her own grave plot she came, & there she sat down,
And heard this voice of sorrow breathed from the hollow pit.

Why cannot the Ear be closed to its own destruction?
Or the glistening Eye to the position of a smile?
Why are Eyelids stor'd with arrows ready drawn,

Where a thousand fighting men in ambush lie?
Or an Eye of gifts & graces show'ring fruits & coined gold?
Why a Tongue impress'd with honey from every wind?
Why an Ear, a whirlpool fierce to draw creations in?
Why a Nostril wide inhaling terror, trembling, & affright?
Why a tender curb upon the youthful burning boy?
Why a little curtain of flesh on the bed of our desire? (*CW,* 130)

Thel has no explanation for our anguish and will not pay the price of Experience. Instead, she rushes back to the world of Innocence, but the attempt to maintain the perspective of Innocence in a fallen world is to lapse into self-deception. As with "To Tirzah," Blake's point in the brief anecdote of Thel is simply that humans can find no satisfaction by means of that false construct of the inhuman world "nature": we must somehow win our way through it to the sustainable Innocence to be found again in Eternity.

Tiriel

Because *Tiriel* (written 1789) employs an earlier attempt at a mythic system, a system whose precise equivalencies have yet to be discovered, the mythic system set forth in *The Book of Urizen* is of limited use in discussing its events. The *Oxford Companion to English Literature* rightly concludes that "the symbolic meaning . . . is obscure."[7] It is clear, nonetheless, that Tiriel represents an image of humanity that reveals not what Blake calls the Human Form Divine but simply decaying mortality, the life of the flesh that Thel accurately saw can offer us only suffering. Tiriel's sons properly reject such a vision as "unworthy to be call'd the father of Tiriel's race"; Ijim (perhaps an early form of Los) similarly denies that Tiriel can be an accurate image of what humanity is; and an enchained Zazel (an early version of the revolutionary Orc) throws stones at the unacceptable "Bald tyrant" Tiriel, whose form imprisons energy in restricting flesh.

Tiriel, like Thel, whose story Blake told the same year, first seeks escape from the fact of mortality; he does so by aid of Mnetha (memory) to seek out a supposed origin for humans in an eternal childhood like the Eden from which conventional Christianity says humanity fell into mortality. For Blake, the Fall is not, of course, a historical event to be visited by memory; instead, it happens moment by moment as we choose to accept the mortality of Tiriel. Even Tiriel himself, the dying natural body, sees at last the inadequacy of a retreat into a false and sentimental past and ends in a lament much like Thel's. And, like Thel, he has found no way to release the Human Form Divine that resides within him. Blake would have us listen, as Tiriel does not, to the imaginative Ijim and to the passionate Zazel, who refuse to accept the limited conception of human potential that Tiriel embodies. If we join in such a refusal, says Blake, we can escape both Thel's fear and Tiriel's. We must learn to say to the merely natural body what Blake said to it in "To Tirzah" in *Songs of Experience:* "Then what have I to do with thee?"

Chapter Eight
The Four Zoas

Of Blake's long narratives, his *Four Zoas,* written 1797–1807, is the one that can be called an "epic," if by that classification we mean a work on a colossal scale, such as Milton's *Paradise Lost* or Dante's *Divine Comedy.* But the subject of *The Four Zoas* is at the same time the most "personal" of Blake's three epics; for what is depicted, by means of the gigantic figures of Blake's myth, is the disintegration and restoration to unity of the faculties that make up the human psyche—Blake's and everyone's. *The Four Zoas* is the flowering of the germ of an epic that is in *The Book of Urizen,* and it is probably the most successful of all the Romantic attempts to turn the epic, usually concerned with the crucial events in a culture or a faith, into a psychologically oriented form that deals with growth, or at least change, in consciousness.

Keats's *Hyperion* and *Fall of Hyperion* raise similar themes, but they remain slim fragments; Wordsworth's *Prelude* is too interested in the biographical processes by which value is created to achieve the universality of myth consistently, although moments in the poem have this power for us; and, though Coleridge's *Ancient Mariner* is admittedly fully achieved mythic art, its scale is tiny compared to Blake's *Four Zoas.* Thus Blake's poem, chaotic as it is in its existence as a manuscript with multiple layers of revision, comes closest to being the Romantic epic that every Romantic poet wanted to write. Blake's *Milton* and his *Jerusalem* lack this particular kind of success because of their concern with specific theological, even "doctrinal," issues.

The Four Zoas was once called *Vala* by Blake, and some have attempted to extract this first version from the confused manuscript. Since it is, however, better critical practice to concentrate on the latest revised version, I use Geoffrey Keynes's version of the full poem but accept David Erdman's argument in his 1965 edition of *The Poetry and Prose* for considering as the later version of "Night the Seventh" the one that Keynes prints as the first (Erdman 1965, 737–39, 755, 762).[1] Of the two titles that Blake considered for the work, certainly the second one, *The Four Zoas,* is the more descriptive, since this poem more thoroughly explores the relationships among the faculties—reason (Urizen), energy (Luvah/Orc), the poetic power (Urthona/Los), and integrative perception

90

(Tharmas)—than any of Blake's other works. The Greek word *zoa*—actually a plural, although Blake used it as a singular—is inadequately translated as "beasts" in the King James version of Revelation. It refers to the figures—ox, lion, eagle, and human—around the throne of the Lamb. Blake chose not to follow the conventional identification of these figures with the four gospels—or, at any rate, he found the use of them as representatives of the human faculties more productive of the myth that he sought to create.

"Night the First"

The Four Zoas is offered as instruction in vision carried to the point where apocalypse threatens:

> long resounding, strong heroic Verse
> Marshall'd in order for the day of Intellectual Battle.
> The heavens quake, the earth was moved & shudder'd, & the mountains
> With all their woods, the streams & valleys wail'd in dismal fear.
> (*CW,* 264)

Such guidance in vision—disruptive of the fixed world we perceive—Blake means to offer, as a deleted passage tells us, to "whosoever reads / If with his intellect he comprehend." Blake reminds us of the psychological unity from which humanity has fallen:

> Four Mighty Ones are in every Man; a Perfect Unity
> Cannot Exist but from the Universal Brotherhood of Eden,
> The Universal Man, to Whom be Glory Evermore. Amen. (*CW,* 264)

Through inspiration (mythically through the Daughters of Beulah), he will relate particularly the fall of the prophetic power in us, the fall of Los who is named Urthona in Eternity:

> Daughter of Beulah, Sing
> His fall into Division & his Resurrection to Unity:
> His fall into the Generation of decay & death, & his
> Regeneration by the Resurrection from the dead. (*CW,* 264)

But the poet will begin with Tharmas, "parent power," a figure that is one of the four zoas that exist in every human being.

Tharmas is that impulse toward unified vision that everyone possesses and whose powers are revealed in the state of Innocence. His emanation, his significant creation, is Enion, who should represent unified and flexible perception. But a terrible error has taken place in our mental habits: we no longer recognize what truly unified perception is; we think that order must mean fixity; and with fixity our creation is separated from us—as we have seen in *The Book of Urizen.* Thus the emanations of the other zoas, cut off from their creators, flee to Tharmas to seek the order that he should represent. But the very separation of the emanations from the zoas is proof that unified perception is now impossible. Clearly, Tharmas has fallen too—has participated in the fall of the zoas.

As a result of the separation, Tharmas's creation, Enion, stands as a judge over him, just as our inhuman theological or scientific systems are allowed to do. She is now—like the church of Blake's day that the Evangelicals were trying to change, like Urizen, and like Satan—an "accuser of sin," for she advocates "Right & Duty instead of Liberty." Tharmas rightly protests Enion's acts of "jealousy" (to apply Blake's usual word for moral rigidity) and voices the same cry that the eighteenth-century writers such as David Hume had started to raise with the recognition that they lived in a world seemingly alien to them: "I am like an atom, / A Nothing, left in darkness; yet I am an identity: / I wish & feel & weep & groan. Ah, terrible! terrible!" (*CW,* 265). For Marxists, this moment of terror in a reified universe is the beginning of the crisis in bourgeois philosophy that will produce what is called Modernism. Yet such an error about the world we inhabit is possible only when we have surrendered our "parent power," when we have forgotten that we create our own environment through the quality of our vision. Thus, as Blake explains mythically, in Eternity "Males immortal live renew'd by female deaths"; that is, emanations do not seek fixity but are content to "revive in spring with music & song" and "in soft / Delight they die." The products of the imagination celebrate the seasons of the mind.

Tharmas has fallen through his acquiescence in the fixity of the emanations. Thus, once the "parent power," the principle of order and unity, he sinks into the sea—into the chaotic world of fallen epistemology. It is the chaos of the material world that the fallen Tharmas comes to represent: the chaos that modern atomic theory agrees is beyond the false order that we think we perceive. Enion draws out the spectre of Tharmas, all that negates his true principle of unity, to form the percep-

tion of those who hold the kind of materialist position that Lenin con-
trasted with the complementary error of philosophical idealism and
called "crude, simple, metaphysical materialism." What follows is therefore the warfare between the perceiver and the content of perception
that characterizes human life in a fallen world:

> The Spectre thus spoke: "Who art thou, Diminutive husk & shell
> Broke from my bonds? I scorn my prison, I scorn & yet I love.
> If thou hast sinn'd & art polluted, know that I am pure
> And unpolluted, & will bring to rigid strict account
> All thy past deeds; hear what I tell thee! mark it well! remember!
> This world is Thine in which thou dwellest; that within thy soul,
> That dark & dismal infinite where Thought roams up & down,
> Is Mine, & there thou goest when with one Sting of my tongue
> Envenom'd thou roll'st inwards to the place whence I emerg'd."
> (*CW*, 268)

Of course, Tharmas is right in knowing that Enion is ultimately subject
to him, but he can no longer make her responsive to her creator. Instead,
he lives with her in a state of constant bickering like that between any
one of us and the environment that we must inhabit.

The coupling of Tharmas, now a principle of materialistic chaos
rather than of order, with Enion, the error of inflexible perception, produces time and space—called Los and Enitharmon, respectively, in
Blake's myth. That Los and Enitharmon are born in this poem of parents
other than those they had in *The Book of Urizen* is not an inconsistency on
Blake's part that is worth pausing over, since materialistic habits of mind
do give birth to the mental categories of time and space and in separation from one another; psychological consistency exists.

Los, despite his prophetic potential, is, like Enitharmon, fully
enslaved to the natural heart and its jealousies:

> Alternate Love & Hate his breast: hers Scorn & jealousy
> In embryon passions; they kiss'd not nor embrac'd for shame & fear.
> His head beam'd light & in his vigorous voice was prophecy.
> He could controll the times & seasons & the days & years;
> She could controll the spaces, regions, desart, flood & forest,

But had no power to weave the Veil of covering for her sins. She
drave the Females all away from Los,
And Los drave the Males from her away. (*CW,* 270–71)

Through the chinks of our cavern-minds light can occasionally shine
because

>   Eno, a daughter of Beulah, took a Moment of Time
> And drew it out to seven thousand years with much care & affliction
> And many tears, & in every year made windows into Eden.
> (*CW,* 270)

Vision, such as the innocent has, stays with humankind to offer some
insight into Eternity. And Infinity still awaits us at either limit: beyond
the universe or within the atom.

Los understands that Albion would not have fallen had he kept the
Divine Image, Jesus and Humanity (for Blake, the Human Form
Divine), before him. Thus, Los and Enitharmon's contentions need continue only "till we have drawn the Lamb of God into a mortal form,"
bringing redemption, as it were, by means of time and space. But
Enitharmon will not worship the Divine Image. Instead, to protect her
status as a fixed form, she is prepared to worship Urizen, the god of jealousy and rigidity:

> Then Enitharmon, redd'ning fierce, stretch'd her immortal hands:
> "Descend, O Urizen, descend with horse & chariot!
> Threaten not me, O visionary; thine the punishment.
> The Human Nature shall no more remain, nor Human acts
> Form the rebellious Spirits of Heaven, but War & Princedom, &
> Victory & Blood." (*CW,* 272)

Urizen, as always, is willing to appear in this role of seeming divinity; and he arrives saying, "Now I am God from Eternity to Eternity."
He offers Los power in the fallen world in exchange for his restraint
of Luvah (Orc), who is always the threat to Urizen's laws and struc-
tures. But, when Los is not willing to cooperate, Urizen suspects the
worst:

Art thou a Visionary of Jesus, the soft delusion of Eternity?
Lo I am God, the terrible destroyer, & not the Saviour.
Why should the Divine Vision compell the sons of Eden
To forego each his own delight, to war against his spectre?
The Spectre is the Man. The rest is only delusion & fancy. (*CW,* 273)

The Spectre, all that Blake feels limits a human being, is humanity itself within Urizen's definition; and Jesus, who so thoroughly transcends such definitions, must be "the soft delusion of Eternity."

Los and Enitharmon, time and space, are wed, a repetition of Tharmas's union with Enion; and, like the previous wedding, theirs helps to make possible the stony world that we see. Neither time nor space exists as a category in the healthy mind; and, because Los and Enitharmon remain separate after their marriage, we can see that they have simply united to torment us in concert. At the wedding feast, the songs are about the dehumanization the human world has undergone: "The Horse is of more value than the Man. The Tyger Fierce / Laughs at the Human form; the Lion mocks & thirsts for blood" (*CW,* 275). The refusal of flexibility on the part of Enion and Enitharmon was similar mockery of what is human. Now the very particles of existence, the particles of our perception, refuse the apocalyptic "Plow & Spade . . . Roller & . . . Harrow," which might be used in "labours of the harvest & the vintage." The energy of Luvah is sealed within these pieces of perception, "The innumerable sons & daughters of Luvah [are] clos'd in furnaces." Our grim desert comes to be the sort of visual environment that we prefer: "There is no City, nor Cornfield, nor Orchard; all is Rock & Sand."

Enion, because she is willing to admit what life in our desert world consists of, can contribute only a lament to the wedding feast:

Why howl the Lion & the Wolf? why do they roam abroad?
Deluded by summer's heat, they sport in enormous love
And cast their young out to the hungry wilds & sandy desarts.

Why is the Sheep given to the knife? the Lamb plays in the Sun:
He starts! he hears the foot of Man! he says: Take thou my wool,
But spare my life: but he knows not that winter cometh fast.
(*CW,* 276)

The mental ground has been readied for the inadequate, violent physical world that comes into being with the marriages of Tharmas and Enion and of Enitharmon and Los. Meanwhile, Albion sinks into sleep, watched over by Jesus.

As an appropriate conclusion to "Night the First," the Daughters of Beulah provide an account of past disorders within Albion. It seems that Urizen and Luvah, reason and energy, had been in conflict, for both were seeking sovereignty. The dispute frightened Urthona, who permitted Enitharmon to escape from him to Tharmas, a lapse that presumably means that Urthona fell into the mistake of seeking order and permanence in his creations. Enitharmon is "murdered" by Enion; that is, she takes on fixity, what we might call life: "such thing was never known / In Eden, that one died a death never to be reviv'd."

One result of the disorders in Albion is that Jerusalem, Albion's emanation, is now fallen too; but she is watched over by the Daughters of Beulah, inspiration always remaining to sustain what should be the true faith of Albion. The mental processes of Albion are, by the end of Night One of *The Four Zoas,* the ultimate of solipsism: "His inward eyes closing from the Divine Vision, & all / His children wandering outside, from his bosom fleeing away" (*CW,* 279). Albion's mental condition is that of the empiricist; he is the victim of the same division between perceiver and object of perception. While he is in such a state, there is no possibility of Jerusalem's restoration to him.

"Night the Second"

The destruction of a healthy unified perception, wherein perceiver and object of perception are one, which was Blake's concern in "Night the First," leads necessarily to the fall of the senses into ratio perception—the subject of the first part of "Night the Second" (which was "Night the First" in *Vala,* Blake's earlier, shorter version of this epic). As "Night the Second" opens, Albion invites Urizen to assume control over his senses:

> Behold these sick'ning Spheres,
> Whence is this voice of Enion that soundeth in my Porches? Take
> thou possession! (*CW,* 280)

Faced with the chaos that results when we create the material world, Albion joins Urizen in longing for fixity. Urizen is as terrified by the chaos of material vision as is Albion: "He saw the indefinite space beneath & his soul shrunk with horror." But his response is not to flee from materialism but to secure a more rigid form of it,

> Petrifying all the Human Imagination into rock & sand.
> Groans ran along Tyburn's brook and along the River of Oxford
> Among the Druid Temples. Albion groan'd on Tyburn's brook:
> Albion gave his loud death groan. The Atlantic Mountains trembled.
> Aloft the Moon fled with a cry: the Sun with streams of blood.
>
> . . . .
>
> Jerusalem came down in a dire ruin over all the Earth,
> She fell cold from Lambeth's Vales in groans & dewy death.
> (*CW,* 281)

Empiricism, based on a view of the mind that assumes the existence of a material world that is both fixed and independent of us, spreads to the universities ("Oxford / Among the Druid Temples") and to the Church[2] ("Jerusalem . . . fell cold from Lambeth's Vales"). Ratio perception fixes the Moon "Aloft" as well as Sun. Urizen is creating the "Mundane Shell" seen by all humans who take flight from the chaos they themselves create; among the types of his victims are the natural man ("Reuben") and the priest ("Levi"):

> Reuben slept on Penmaenmawr & Levi slept on Snowdon.
> Their eyes, their ears, nostrils & tongues roll outward, they behold
> What is within now seen without; they are raw to the hungry wind.
> (*CW,* 281)

Luvah (Orc), the energy that Urizen fears, is imprisoned within the physical world, "cast into the Furnaces of affliction & sealed." There he is tormented by Vala, properly his emanation, but now the mocking "Nature" that places limits on energy. The suffering Luvah is, however, now fallen too; and he feels that his fall was carried out "to deliver all the sons of God / From bondage of the Human form." He is, Blake tells us, "Reasoning from the loins in the unreal forms of Ulro's night." His mental powers are perverted by his mistaken materialism.

Ratio perception is established, and only a few individuals dare question it:

With trembling horror pale, aghast the Children of Man
Stood on the infinite Earth & saw these visions in the air,
In waters & in earth beneath; they cried to one another,
"What! are we terrors to one another? Come, O brethren, wherefore
Was this wide Earth spread all abroad? not for wild beasts to roam."
(*CW,* 283)

They ask the proper question—the one that Blake's poem "The Tyger"
invites us to ask—in demanding to know why we must inhabit a desert
where "wild beasts . . . roam." Most people, however, accept the ratio
world, its values, and its forms of life, which include the marketplace in
which a commodified reality is bought and sold:

But many stood silent, & busied in their families.
And many said, "We see no Visions in the darksom air.
Measure the course of that sulphur orb that lights the darksom day;
Set stations on this breeding Earth & let us buy & sell."
Others arose & schools erected, forming Instruments
To measure out the course of heaven. (*CW,* 283)

With "compasses" and "strong scales," their world of fallen vision is
meted out to them. The senses (as in the description at the end of *The
Book of Thel*) become only a torment; for they trap our energies and close
worlds of delight: "In cruel delight they trap the listeners, & in cruel
delight / Bind them, condensing the strong energies into little compass"
(*CW,* 284). This world, shaped by Urizen in his fear, is accepted as a
comfortable "common-sense" stay by most people; and we remember
Sam Johnson's kicking a stone to refute Bishop Berkeley.

"Night the Second" concludes with a review of the condition of the
emanations of the four zoas. Earlier (*CW,* 282), Luvah has told us that
"Urizen, who was Faith & certainty, is chang'd to Doubt." Accordingly,
he is now separated from Ahania, his emanation. Ahania would represent wisdom if Urizen still possessed her, and Vala would represent fulfilled emotional life. Instead, Vala finds herself in torment like that of the
women in *Visions of the Daughters of Albion:* "We are made to turn the
wheel for water, / To carry the heavy basket on our scorched shoulders"
(*CW,* 285–86). Enitharmon should represent the creative acts of Los, but
she mocks him instead as the threatening space that the artist must

overcome: "for thou art mine, / Created for my will, my slave, tho' strong, tho' I am weak" (*CW,* 288). And Enion, who should represent fulfilled perception, is now trapped within the vision of Experience, which Blake here defines in terms of the capitalist marketplace:

What is the price of Experience? do men buy it for a song?
Or wisdom for a dance in the street? No, it is bought with the price
Of all that a man hath, his house, his wife, his children.
Wisdom is sold in the desolate market where none come to buy,
And in the wither'd field where the farmer plows for bread in vain.
(*CW,* 290)

In the cries of the four "females," we find a full sense of what the shattering of our vision of Eternity has cost us.

"Night the Third"

"Night the Third" is the shortest of the sections that make up *The Four Zoas,* and it consists primarily of a flashback narrative that is provided by Ahania, who is speaking to Urizen. Urizen rightly fears that he cannot forever sustain the mundane shell that he caused to be created for ratio perception; but Ahania reminds him of his rise to power over Albion. Albion, because of his "wearied intellect," has, in effect, deified Urizen, the rational faculty—a process repeated by the thinkers of the Enlightenment or by anyone who envisions a lawmaker God:

Idolatrous to his own Shadow, words of Eternity uttering:
"O I am nothing when I enter into judgment with thee.
If thou withdraw thy breath I die & vanish into Hades;
If thou dost lay thine hand upon me, behold I am silent;
If thou withhold thine hand I perish like a fallen leaf.
O I am nothing, & to nothing must return again.
If thou withdraw thy breath, behold I am oblivion." (*CW,* 293)

The idea of holiness has been externalized by Albion, who forgets that all deities reside in the human breast. The result of the deification of the rational faculty is the rejection of the energetic: "Then frown'd the Fallen

Man [Albion] & put forth Luvah from his presence." Rejected energy petrifies into the deceptive natural heart:

> Luvah and Vala
> Went down the Human Heart, where Paradise & its joys abounded,
> In jealous fears, in fury & rage, & flames roll'd round their fervid feet,
> And the vast form of Nature like a Serpent play'd before them.
> (*CW*, 294)

The human heart, which should be a world of delight that allows participation in Eternity, is filled with the torments of jealousy that demand fixity and the "external world" called "Nature."

Urizen finds no comfort in hearing again how he was elevated and how Luvah was demoted. He is still fearful, and his separated emanation, Ahania, his own "wisdom," now reflects only his own weakness: "thou hast risen with thy moist locks into a wat'ry image / Reflecting all my indolence, my weakness & my death" (*CW*, 295). He casts her off: a despairing suicidal act that the rational mind was often driven to in the eighteenth century and afterwards. We think especially of Lord Byron, the Romantic poet who, through characters like Cain and Manfred, most strongly expressed our resentment at the limited scope that human knowledge of the world offers us; but Byron rejected all possibility of wisdom found through the imagination by saying that it only reveals how "of its own beauty is the mind diseased, / And fevers into false creation."

With the separation of Ahania from Urizen, Tharmas—who should represent our unified perception—has completed his metamorphosis into the total chaos represented by the sea, the best emblem of the chaotic "atomic" world we choose to inhabit. Tharmas's voice is now blubbering confusion:

> My skull riven into filaments, my eyes into sea jellies
> Floating upon the tide wander bubbling & bubbling,
> Uttering my lamentations & begetting little monsters
> Who sit mocking upon the little pebbles of the tide
> In all my rivers & on dried shells that the fish
> Have quite forsaken. O fool! fool! to lose my sweetest bliss.
> (*CW*, 296)

Enion, who should be the world that is seen by unified perception, longs to return to Tharmas; but he cannot repossess the healthy state of vision that he once had:

Why does thy piteous face Evanish like a rainy cloud
Melting, a shower of falling tears, nothing but fears! Enion,
Substanceless, voiceless, weeping, vanish'd, nothing but tears! Enion,
Art thou for ever vanish'd from the wat'ry eyes of Tharmas?
(*CW*, 297)

The clear, definite vision of Eternity has been replaced by the watery vistas of ratio perception and by the material world it creates. Only Urizen's fear suggests that anything could undo this fallen world.

"Night the Fourth"

In "Night the Fourth," Los, the "prophetic boy" (*CW*, 292) who is feared by Urizen, is forced to put his imagination into the service of ratio perception and ultimately to give shape to Urizen as ruler of this world. Tharmas starts this process by producing from the division of Los and Enitharmon the Spectre of Urthona who represents everything that limits the imaginative poet. The Spectre of Urthona responds to the threats that are most destructive of the artist who would transcend this world. Thus Tharmas gains his obedience through terrifying him with images of death: "If thou refusest, dash'd abroad on all / My waves, thy limbs shall separate in stench & rotting, & thou / Become a prey to all my demons of despair & hope" (*CW*, 299).

The poet who hears these threats responds by seeking the false order of, say, a British eighteenth-century poet. Fear, originating in the fallen natural heart, drives Los into fixing the creations of Urizen as he did in *The Book of Urizen* (and indeed Blake borrows most of his description of the process from that work). Thus even art has been rendered subservient to a false epistemology, and the artist seems a correspondingly lessened figure: "[Los] became what he beheld: / He became what he was doing: he was himself transform'd" (*CW*, 305). The process was called Neoclassicism in literary history.

But the fall has reached its limits at this point—although specific solidifications of error, such as Natural Religion and "Nature" itself, are yet to appear. Jesus has set limits in every individual's psychology beyond which one cannot fall: the limits are necessarily there, of course, since human beings, despite their fallen nature, are innately divine. Thus:

> The Saviour mild & gentle bent over the corse of Death,
> Saying, "If ye will Believe, your Brother shall rise again."
> And first he found the Limit of Opacity, & nam'd it Satan,
> In Albion's bosom, for in every human bosom these limits stand.
> And next he found the Limit of Contraction, & named it Adam,
> While yet those beings were not born nor knew of good or Evil.
> (*CW*, 304)

Humanity will not perceive a world more opaque, more closed to Eternity, than that which Urizen now gives us. (Urizen's fallen name is, of course, Satan, the god of this world and the Accuser of Sin.) Humans will not shrink beyond the forms our bodies now possess: we will not fall ("contract") beyond the state reached by Adam. From this base at least, Los—though now a victim of the Spectre of Urthona, his own fears— can work for renewal.

"Night the Fifth"

"Night the Fifth" pictures the binding of energy within the natural world that is, at the same time, the entry of apocalyptic hope into our world of time and space. As the Daughters of Beulah had said at the end of "Night the Fourth," Jesus appears "cloth'd in Luvah's garments that we may behold [Him] / And live." Los and Enitharmon, separated and petrified, "Shrunk into fixed space . . . unexpansive," live in the darkness and cold of a Urizenic world. Into this winter season Luvah (Orc) is born, as was Jesus at Christmas. But, as always, Luvah-Orc is the revolutionary power; he represents energy that demands its rightful place in our mental universe, and is such a threat that his own parents must resist him. He enacts what we, long after Blake, have come to see as a fundamental act of adolescent rebellion:

> But when fourteen summers & winters had revolved over
> Their solemn habitation, Los beheld the ruddy boy

Embracing his bright mother, & beheld malignant fires
In his young eyes, discerning plain that Orc plotted his death.
Grief rose upon his ruddy brows; a tightening girdle grew
Around his bosom like a bloody cord; in secret sobs
He burst it, but next morn another girdle succeeds
Around his bosom. Every day he view'd the fiery youth
With silent fear. (*CW,* 307)

Los is bound in the girdle of jealousy, which means not simply sexual jealousy, but the fear of the loss of order upon which jealousy is based. Orc's very presence may be seen as "warring with the waves of Tharmas & Snows of Urizen" and, therefore, as a threat to the Los who, in "Night the Fourth," "became what he beheld." As in *The Book of Urizen,* Los chains Orc, thereby tying him to the natural cycle, an act that means that now only the violent harrowing that destroys the "physical" can bring about our return to Eternity (as it does in the later books of *The Four Zoas*). In the process from which Thel fled, Orc has the torments of the natural heart:

Lo, the young limbs had stucken root into the rock, & strong
Fibres had from the Chain of jealousy inwove themselves
In a swift vegetation round the rock & round the Cave
And over the immortal limbs of the terrible fiery boy.
In vain they strove now to unchain, in vain with bitter tears
To melt the chain of jealousy. (*CW,* 309)

The howling of the energetic Orc for freedom shakes the world and hints at apocalypse: "Urizen trembled . . . to hear the howling terror" (*CW,* 310).

Urizen now regrets the loss of Eternity and offers a weary lamentation (*CW,* 310–11). But he must nevertheless set out to assess the threat represented by the shaking of the world by the furious Luvah-Orc: "I will arise, Explore these dens, & find that deep pulsation / That shakes my cavern with strong shudders; perhaps this is the night / Of Prophecy, & Luvah hath burst his way from Enitharmon" (*CW,* 311). "Night the Sixth" offers the record of his quest.

"Night the Sixth"

At the outset of "Night the Sixth," Urizen encounters "three terrific women," who turn out to be his own daughters. Most commentators take them to be representative of the loins, the heart, and the brain. If these identifications are the right ones, they should represent the visionary potential carried in our lives by sex, emotion, and imagination. Not surprisingly, Urizen offers them "chains," "cords , and "whips" for an enslavement like that endured by the Daughters of Albion "that they may worship terrors & obey the violent" (*CW,* 313). When we see these women again, they are (like Vala) tormenters of Orc and are the repressors of energy through their advocacy of Moral Virtue.

Next, Urizen encounters Tharmas, who is in such a state of despair over the quality of his perception that he seeks a death pact with Urizen:

> The Body of Man is given to me. I seek in vain to destroy,
> For still it surges forth in fish & monsters of the deeps,
> And in these monstrous forms I Live in an Eternal woe,
> And thou, O Urizen, art fall'n, never to be deliver'd.
> Withhold thy light from me for ever, & I will withhold
> From thee thy food; so shall we cease to be, & all our sorrows
> End, & the Eternal Man no more renew beneath our power.
> (*CW,* 313)

Since there is no body distinct from the soul, as Blake has told us, Tharmas, as keeper of Man's body, is the custodian of perception. Yet Tharmas's perception is like ours; it is full of unaccountable outbreaks of energy ("fish & monsters of the deeps") that should tell us that we have imposed a false order on the world. Urizen, who simply ignores Tharmas's pleas and threats, seeks for himself further abstractions with which to close the gaps in perception of which Tharmas complains. As a first step, Urizen, like a good empiricist, investigates the human condition:

> Scar'd at the sound of their own sigh that seems to shake the immense
> They wander Moping, in their heart a sun, a dreary moon,
> A Universe of fiery constellations in their brain,
> An earth of wintry woe beneath their feet, & round their loins

Waters or winds or clouds or brooding lightnings & pestilential
plagues.
Beyond the bounds of their own self their senses cannot penetrate:
As the tree knows what is outside of its leaves & bark
And yet it drinks the summer joy & fears the winter sorrow.
(*CW,* 314)

Falsely closed within themselves, human beings, Blake believes, find
only sorrow. Yet there are everywhere proofs of the inadequacy of their
solipsistically formed universe: "Then he beheld the forms of tygers & of
Lions, dishumaniz'd men." A human world awaits each of us outside the
caverns into which we have closed ourselves.

Urizen tries to conduct the sort of apocalyptic questioning that
Blake's "Tyger" would urge us to undertake: "Oft would he stand &
question a fierce scorpion glowing with gold; / In vain; the terror heard
not" (*CW,* 315). Urizen does not know how to pursue such a quest for
truth: the empirical method yields no real answers to the "idiot
Questioner" who employs it. Since Urizen cannot free humankind ("He
could not take their fetters off"), he creates scientific explanations of
their condition, "Creating many a Vortex, fixing many a Science in the
deep." Like the true empiricist, like Bromion in *Visions of the Daughters of
Albion,* he longs for better conditions of "observation":

But Urizen said: "Can I not leave this world of Cumbrous wheels,
Circle o'er Circle, nor on high attain a void
Where self sustaining I may view all things beneath my feet?
Or sinking thro' these Elemental wonders, swift to fall,
I thought perhaps to find an End, a world beneath of voidness
Whence I might travel round the outside of this dark confusion."
(*CW,* 316–17)

He is certain that, given the right sort of laboratory conditions, he
can explain our anguish to us. For, as post-Newtonian humanity soon
knew, our world seems only the ruins of Paradise:

"O what a world is here, unlike those climes of bliss
Where my sons gather'd round my knees! O, thou poor ruin'd
world!

Thou horrible ruin! once like me thou wast all glorious,
And now like me partaking desolate thy master's lot." (*CW,* 317)

He creates bigger abstractions, fancier systems:

So he began to form of gold, silver & iron
And brass, vast instruments to measure out the immense & fix
The whole into another world better suited to obey
His will, where none should dare oppose his will, himself being
King Of All, & all futurity be bound in his vast chain.
And the Sciences were fix'd & the Vortexes began to operate
On all the sons of men, & every human soul terrified
At the turning wheels of heaven shrunk away inward, with'ring
away. (*CW,* 317)

"A living Mantle adjoined to his life & growing from his soul," his new
science stretches as "the Web of Urizen." He has spun out explanations
of all that he sees and sits at the center a grim and hoary spider.

Finally, the empiricist approaches the possible gap in his web represented by the fierce Orc whose anguish first started Urizen on his scientific quest. But Urizen cannot now approach Orc, for even such
demented characters as Tharmas and the Spectre of Urthona intervene
to protect him. Instead, as "Night the Sixth" ends, Urizen retreats to his
scientist's spider web, where the planets whirl about him:

Then Urizen arose upon the wind, back many a mile
Retiring into his dire Web, scattering fleecy snows:
As he ascended, howling loud, the Web vibrated strong,
From heaven to heaven, from globe to globe. In vast excentric paths
Compulsive roll'd the Comets at his dread command, the dreary way
Falling with wheel impetuous down among Urthona's vales
And round red Orc; returning back to Urizen, gorg'd with blood.
Slow roll the massy Globes at his command, & slow o'erwheel
The dismal squadrons of Urthona weaving the dire Web
In their progressions, & preparing Urizen's path before him.
(*CW,* 319–20)

We have filled our heads with webs like these, says Blake, and we use them to "see" the sky with. But such systems still do not account for the possible eruption of Luvah-Orc—or for the coming of Jesus.

"Night the Seventh," Revised Version

As Geoffrey Keynes points out, "Blake wrote two versions of Night the Seventh, but did not finally reject either" (*CW,* 320). The version printed first by Keynes as having been written earlier—but considered by subsequent scholars to be the later in date of composition—moves from the preceding "Night the Sixth" with the more natural transition and introduces concepts of considerable value for our understanding of the concluding nights of *The Four Zoas.* It begins with Urizen's rising from his solipsistic web of stars to look into another's flaming rich bosom, the act that Orleans summoned us to in *The French Revolution* as an antidote for our desire to be lawgivers. This kingdom is Orc's:

> But Urizen silent descended to the Caves of Orc & saw
> A Cavern'd Universe of flaming fire; the horses of Urizen
> Here bound to fiery mangers, furious dash their golden hoofs,
> Striking fierce sparkles from their brazen fetters fierce his lions
> Howl in the burning dens; his tygers roam in the redounding smoke
> In forests of affliction; the adamantine scales of justice
> Consuming in the raging lamps of mercy, pour'd in rivers.
> The holy oil rages thro' all the cavern'd rocks; fierce flames
> Dance on the rivers & the rocks; howling & drunk with fury
> The plow of ages & the golden harrow wade thro' fields
> Of goary blood; the immortal seed is nourish'd for the slaughter.
> The bulls of Luvah, breathing fire, bellow on burning pastures
> Round howling Orc, whose awful limbs cast forth red smoke & fire,
> That Urizen approached not near but took his seat on a rock
> And rang'd his books around him, brooding Envious over Orc.
> (*CW,* 320)

What Urizen sees, of course, is a world of pure energy, energy of a sort that consumes Urizenic "scales of justice" and threatens to bring out the plow and harrow that will tear apart Urizen's ratio-perception world.

But, since Orc is himself in fetters, Urizen can safely sit to watch his torments.

Urizen's jealousy, which has already wrought so many evils, is now the parent of the Tree of Mystery that represents all religions that repress energy and imagination. Orc, who is forced to circle this tree, assumes the serpent form of priestcraft (see, for instance, *The French Revolution*) as a punishment for his continuing assertions to Urizen that his "fierce fires are better than [Urizen's] snows." The daughters of Urizen hold Orc, always a potentially revolutionary energy, by the arts of "Moral Virtue" that serve only to support privilege and the existing economic system:

> Compell the poor to live upon a Crust of Bread, by soft mild arts.
> Smile when they frown, frown when they smile; & when a man looks pale
> With labour & abstinence, say he looks healthy & happy;
> And when his children sicken, let them die; there are enough
> Born, even too many, & our Earth will be overrun
> Without these arts. If you would make the poor live with temper,
> With pomp give every crust of bread you give; with gracious cunning
> Magnify small gifts; reduce the man to want a gift, & then give with pomp.
> Say he smiles if you hear him sigh. If pale, say he is ruddy.
> Preach temperance: say he is overgorg'd & drowns his wit
> In strong drink, tho' you know that bread & water are all
> He can afford. Flatter his wife, pity his children, till we can
> Reduce all to our will, as spaniels are taught with art. (*CW,* 323)

Through such arts Orc is transformed, against his will, to serve as Urizen's priest so "that he might draw all human forms / Into submission to his will." The perversion of the revolutionary Orc into the "sneaking serpent" of priestcraft is instructively ironic because it was Orc who drove the priests into their "reptile coverts" in *America.* The emergence of priestcraft in this way is, however, a recurring event in Blake's myth, meant to convey the misuse of human potential introduced in separating rational subject from alien object and thereby initiating the division of labor; Marx makes the same observation about the origin of priests.

Los has, in the meantime, lost Enitharmon, whose shadow now flees to the Tree of Mystery to start the process by which a world perceived as "space" can be joined to the idea of religion and form Natural Religion. Urizen had wished that his daughters might "Draw down Enitharmon to the Spectre of Urthona, / And let him have dominion over Los," and he seems to be having his way as Enitharmon and the Spectre of Urthona mate at the Tree of Mystery to bring into being Vala, who will ultimately be the full embodiment of Natural Religion. (In mental terms, such union and birth mean that all that limits the imagination has merged with a false concept of space to produce the assumptions behind the characteristic theology of the eighteenth century.) But Urizen doesn't get his way entirely; for the Spectre of Urthona, who reveals his own sense of inadequacy in his conversation with Enitharmon, offers to join with Los in producing visionary works of art:

If we unite in one, another better world will be
Open'd within your heart & loins & wondrous brain,
Threefold, as it was in Eternity, & this, the fourth Universe,
Will be Renew'd by the three & consummated in Mental fires;
(*CW,* 329)

The works they produce together will be only threefold, subject to the limits of opacity and contraction ("having a Limit Twofold nam'd Satan & Adam"); but they will bring the imagination to the borders of Eternity again.

Enitharmon tries to introduce doubt into Los's mind by arguing for "accusation of sin" and the doctrine of the atonement, "That without a ransom I could not be sav'd from Eternal death." But Los is now too strong to accept these deceptions from the Tree of Mystery. He can even provide the Blakean response: "Turn inwardly thine Eyes & there behold the Lamb of God Clothed in Luvah's robes of blood descending to redeem" (*CW,* 330). Clearly he is ready to take on the role of visionary artist, and, as he does, so he compels even the cooperation of the recalcitrant spatial world: "And first he drew a line upon the walls of shining heaven, / And Enitharmon tinctur'd it with beams of blushing love. / It remain'd permanent, a lovely form, inspir'd, divinely human" (*CW,* 332).

Such works of art are produced for our benefit, and they serve as "counterparts" for our visionary yearnings that otherwise have no outlet. Blake's own art, suggested here by the drawing of the visionary line and by the subsequent coloring of the outline, has the same intention. These products of the imagination are loved by Los, who refuses "to Sacrifice their infant limbs," and he, with Blake, is now ready to lead us toward the apocalypse through the concluding nights of *The Four Zoas*. Already, in fact, his art has transformed all that is fearful in Urizen into the easily recognizable figure of Satan; and, though finding "his Enemy Urizen now in his hands," Los can feel "love & not hate." Soon all the energy that Urizen (now Satan) feared at the outset of "Night the Seventh" will be released.

"Night the Eighth"

"Night the Eighth" of *The Four Zoas* is centrally concerned with the fall of the English church into the delusions of natural theology, but it simultaneously depicts the renewed presence of Jesus in the hearts of the Inspired. As a result, it mirrors the hopes for revolutionary change in both theology and politics that Blake shared with the Evangelicals on one hand and republicans on the other. There are, accordingly, signs of Albion's awakening as "Night the Eighth" opens:

> Man began
> To wake upon the Couch of Death; he sneezed seven times;
> A tear of blood dropped from either eye; again he repos'd
> In the Saviour's arms, in the arms of tender mercy & loving kind-
> ness. (*CW*, 341)

Los is again able to "behold the Divine Vision" through the stony fallen world that we must inhabit. And Enitharmon now labors to provide the material "counterparts" of visionary art for human beings who have fallen into single vision. The false dichotomy of subject and object is overcome in the art object in which the human creator and the created object have engaged.

Urizen is driven to a final effort by these new threats to his realm. With the connivance of priestcraft ("Communing with the Serpent of Orc in dark dissimulation"), he creates the totally solipsistic vision toward which his self-enclosure has always tended:

> a Shadowy hermaphrodite, black & opake;
> The soldiers nam'd it Satan, but he was yet unform'd & vast
> Hermaphroditic it at length became, hiding the Male
> Within as in a Tabernacle, Abominable, Deadly. (*CW,* 343)

The confusion between "perceiver" and "perceived" that characterizes the empirical method results in a hermaphrodite world that confuses the "man" and his emanation. Los resists the formation of such a world, closed as it would be to vision, and struggles to humanize its particles:

> They humanize in the fierce battle, where in direful pain
> Troop by troop the beastial droves rend one another, sounding loud
> The instruments of sound; & troop by troop, in human forms, they urge
> The dire confusion till the battle faints; those that remain
> Return in pangs & horrible convulsions to their beastial state;
> For the monsters of the Elements, Lions or Tygers or Wolves,
> Sound loud the howling music Inspir'd by Los & Enitharmon, sounding loud; terrific men
> They seem to one another, laughing terrible among the banners.
> (*CW,* 344)

The imperfect process of humanization leads, as always, to the formation of terrifying tigers and other "monsters" who are the proof of the inadequacy of our vision. These terrors form Urizen's world:

> And Urizen gave life & sense by his immortal power
> To all his Engines of deceit: that linked chains might run
> Thro' ranks of war spontaneous: & that hooks & boring screws
> Might act according to their forms by innate cruelty.
> He formed also harsh instruments of sound
> To grate the soul into destruction, or to inflame with fury
> The spirits of life, to pervert all the faculties of sense
> Into their own destruction, if perhaps he might avert
> His own despair even at the cost of every thing that breathes.
> (*CW,* 344)

This world is the painful one of the senses from which Thel fled but in which the empiricist delights.

Vala, our knowledge of the natural world, takes on the "enormous Sciences of Urizen" to become the scientific world view of the eighteenth century. Then she is wed to the Tree of Mystery to become, completely and at last, natural religion. Meanwhile, the imaginative acts of all fallen humans ("the dead") take shape as Jerusalem:

> And Enitharmon named the Female, Jerusalem the holy.
> Wond'ring, she saw the Lamb of God within Jerusalem's Veil;
> The Divine Vision seen within the inmost deep recess
> Of fair Jerusalem's bosom in a gently beaming fire. (*CW,* 346)

From Jerusalem will come Jesus to overthrow "the dark Satanic body" whose formation we have seen.

Satan acts to protect himself and to counter the efforts of the imagination. One method he relies on is identifying all that is visionary as sin: "to . . . reveal / Naked of their clothing the poor spectres before the accusing heavens." To replace the visionary garments, he brings "webs of torture, / Mantles of despair, girdles of bitter compunction, shoes of indolence, / Veils of ignorance"; and all of these are too often the garb of those suffering under the weight of imputed sin. All their anguish contributes to the preservation of natural religion: "this Lake is form'd from the tears & sighs & death sweat of the Victims / Of Urizen's laws, to irrigate the roots of the tree of Mystery" (*CW,* 347). Satan is now all that opposes or seeks to negate Jerusalem, "Being multitudes of tyrant Men in union blasphemous / Against the Divine image, Congregated assemblies of wicked men." But he can be no match for Jesus, who is willing to work through the Satanic world—"Assume the dark Satanic body in the Virgin's womb"—and to bring it to apocalypse.

A corrupt institutionalized religion (Rahab) and the natural world (Tirzah) on which it is founded assert their power over Jesus in the Crucifixion:

> Thus was the Lamb of God condemn'd to Death.
> They nail'd him upon the tree of Mystery, weeping over him
> And then mocking & then worshipping, calling him Lord & King.
> Sometimes as twelve daughters lovely, & sometimes as five

They stood in beaming beauty, & sometimes as one, even Rahab
Who is Mystery, Babylon the Great, the Mother of Harlots.
(*CW,* 349)

Jerusalem, who should represent the vital faith of Albion, misinterprets
the Crucifixion and gives birth to a religion that is a cult of death:

> let us build
> A Sepulcher & worship Death in fear while yet we live:
> Death! God of All! from whom we rise, to whom we all return:
> And Let all Nations of the Earth worship at the Sepulcher
> With Gifts & Spices, with lamps rich emboss'd, jewels & gold.
> (*CW,* 349)

At first, Los also misunderstands and, "despairing of Life Eternal," buries
Jesus.

But Los recovers his sight quickly, recognizes Rahab for what she is,
and offers the history of the fall of humanity to demonstrate his visionary understanding. Urizen, meanwhile, becomes petrified as a result of
his petrified vision, "his human form a Stone, / A form of Senseless Stone
remain'd." Tharmas and Urthona turn over their respective "Power" and
"Strength" to Los, who will carry on their apocalyptic strivings for them.
Ahania and Enion return to lament our fallen condition again, but Enion
looks forward to the humanization of the universe:

> The Lamb of God has rent the Veil of Mystery, soon to return
> In Clouds & Fires around the rock & the Mysterious tree.
> And as the seed waits Eagerly watching for its flower & fruit,
> Anxious its little soul looks out into the clear expanse
> To see if hungry winds are abroad with their invisible army,
> So Man looks out in tree & herb & fish & bird & beast
> Collecting up the scatter'd portions of his immortal body
> Into the Elemental forms of every thing that grows. (*CW,* 355)

All the principals have gathered for the tremendous finale that Blake
has prepared. Natural Religion takes on the precise historical character
that it had when Blake wrote this poem: Jerusalem is "Captive . . . by

delusive arts impell'd / To worship Urizen's Dragon form, to offer her own Children / Upon the bloody Altar." Rahab, cast into defining flames, becomes a Phoenix of Error: "The Ashes of Mystery began to animate; they call'd it Deism / And Natural Religion; as of old, so now anew began / Babylon again in Infancy, call'd Natural Religion" (*CW,* 357). Error has now been identified; and Los, the imaginative artist, is, like Blake, ready to counter it.

"Night the Ninth"

"Night the Ninth" of *The Four Zoas* returns us at last to Eternity. The process begins when Los, still mourning the apparent loss of Jesus to the sepulcher, experiences the fear that is vision:

> Terrified at Non Existence,
> For such they deem'd the death of the body, Los his vegetable hands
> Outstretch'd; his right hand, branching out in fibrous strength,
> Siez'd the Sun; His left hand, like dark roots, cover'd the Moon,
> And tore them down, cracking the heavens across from immense to
> immense. (*CW,* 357)

What Los does here is what any of us could do if we would. Because he has proved human superiority over "space" and "time," the Spectre of Enitharmon and the Spectre of Urthona also fall and have "their bodies buried in the ruins of the Universe." Urizen's books unroll, and the serpent Orc "began to Consume in fierce raving fire."

The Last Judgment is at once under way because, as Blake said elsewhere, "Whenever any Individual Rejects Error & Embraces Truth, a Last Judgment passes upon that Individual" (*CW,* 613). When Los, our imaginative faculty, refuses to accept the Newtonian world, we are lifted toward Eternity: "from the clotted gore & from the hollow den / Start forth the trembling millions into flames of mental fire, / Bathing their limbs in the bright visions of Eternity" (*CW,* 358). The institutions that had been founded upon a fallen epistemology come at once to an end: tyrants lose their power, and the Tree of Mystery is immediately consumed. And at last Albion comes fully awake.

Albion is now clear-sighted enough to castigate Urizen—now a stony dragon—for his errors. Urizen responds at once by rejecting the jealous mental habit that had tried to control "futurity" by making laws:

Then Go, O dark futurity! I will cast thee forth from these
Heavens of my brain, nor will I look upon futurity more.
I cast futurity away, & turn my back upon that void
Which I have made; for lo! futurity is in this moment. (*CW,* 361–62)

With this act, he frees himself of his long characteristic "snows" and "his aged mantles":

Then, glorious bright, Exulting in his joy,
He sounding rose into the heavens in naked majesty,
In radiant Youth; when Lo! like garlands in the Eastern sky
When vocal may comes dancing from the East, Ahania came
Exulting in her flight, as when a bubble rises up
On to the surface of a lake, Ahania rose in joy. (*CW,* 362)

The union with Ahania is somewhat premature, since the final human-ization of the world has not yet taken place; but Ahania *will* soon be restored to the reborn Urizen.

As the Universe humanizes, the once oppressive Newtonian shapes are seen for what they are—the body of Satan that crucifies Jesus and the corrupters of theology. Thus they begin to reform as well: "They see him whom they have pierc'd, they wail because of him, / They magnify themselves no more against Jerusalem" (*CW,* 364). Every human's perception is improving. Luvah and Vala return to the loins of Albion where they belong, and Tharmas and Enion are restored to the pastoral world of Innocence that healthy perception once knew, a fit world for "the lovely eyes of Tharmas & the Eyes of Enion." Thus any aspect of our vision that had seemed at all alienated is now filled with joy:

The roots shoot thick thro' the solid rocks, bursting their way
They cry out in joys of existence; the broad stems
Rear on the mountains stem after stem; the scaly newt creeps
From the stone, & the armed fly springs from the rocky crevice,
The spider, The bat burst from the harden'd slime, crying
To one another: "What are we, & whence is our joy & delight?
Lo, the little moss begins to spring, & the tender weed

Creeps round our secret nest." Flocks brighten the Mountains,
Herds throng up the Valley, wild beasts fill the forests. (*CW,* 373)

And it is Tharmas, restored perception, who can announce the end of the
religions based on false epistemology and point to the eradication of the
social evils that those religions wrought: "Mystery is no more" (*CW,*
375).

The physical world that we have known undergoes a crushing into
"Human Wine" as all the zoas, now their eternal selves, join in the work.
Eternity is present again:

> The Sun has left his blackness & has found a fresher morning,
> And the mild moon rejoices in the clear & cloudless night,
> And Man walks forth from midst of the fires: the evil is all
> consum'd.
> His eyes behold the Angelic spheres arising night & day;
> The stars consum'd like a lamp blown out, & in their stead, behold
> The Expanding Eyes of Man behold the depths of wondrous worlds!
> One Earth, one sea beneath; nor Erring Globes wander, but Stars
> Of fire rise up nightly from the Ocean; & one Sun
> Each morning, like a New born Man, issues with songs & joy
> Calling the Plowman to his Labour & the Shepherd to his rest.
> He walks upon the Eternal Mountains, raising his heavenly voice.
> Conversing with the Animal forms of wisdom night & day,
> That, risen from the Sea of fire, renew'd walk o'er the Earth,
> For Tharmas brought his flocks upon the hills, & in the Vales
> Around the Eternal Man's bright tent, the little children play
> Among the wooly flocks. The hammer of Urthona sounds
> In the deep caves beneath; his limbs renew'd, his Lions roar
> Around the Furnaces & in Evening sport upon the plains.
> They raise their faces from the Earth, conversing with the Man.
> (*CW,* 379)

This fully human world of restored perception resembles the pastoral
world of Innocence, but it is now not to be threatened by our entry into
Experience. The once terrifying sun is human, "a New born Man," and

the Lions we once feared as we did the Tyger now chat with us. The life of mortal warfare is done with, and there is now only the pleasure of "intellectual war," the art and science of Eternity: "The war of swords departed now, / The dark religions are departed & sweet Science reigns" (*CW,* 379). "The dark Religions," which spoke of atonement and the accusation of sin, are now replaced by vision. Humanity has awakened to its own divinity.

Chapter Nine
Manuscript Poems

The poetry of Blake that remained unpublished and unilluminated included not only the epic *The Four Zoas* but also a large number of shorter manuscript poems that are both lyric and satiric. Some of these are indeed variants of poems used in *Innocence* or *Experience* or elsewhere, but a few have long earned a place of their own in collections of Blake's poetry. One of the best known is Blake's fierce rejection of Voltaire and Rousseau—and of all science based on empiricism and a crude materialism:

> Mock on, Mock on Voltaire, Rousseau:
> Mock on, Mock on: 'tis all in vain!
> You throw the sand against the wind,
> And the wind blows it back again.
>
> And every sand becomes a Gem
> Reflected in the beams divine;
> Blown back they blind the mocking Eye,
> But still in Israel's paths they shine.
>
> The Atoms of Democritus
> And Newton's Particles of light
> Are sands upon the Red sea shore,
> Where Israel's tents do shine so bright. (*CW,* 418)

Despite the claims to scientific understanding made by Voltaire, Rousseau, and Newton, the world they describe is not the world of human experience. Theirs is in fact the "crude, simple, metaphysical materialism" to which, supporting a Marxist understanding of the relationship between subject and object, Lenin would object (Lenin, 38, 363).

Another important manuscript poem is the defiantly shapeless "Auguries of Innocence," which offers a strong statement of Blake's view that a recognition of the inadequacies of the world we inhabit is a summons to imaginative vision and reminds us that "We are led to Believe a Lie / When we see not Thro' the Eye" (*CW,* 433). But none of the other manuscript poems makes the demand for attention in its own terms that is made by each of three mysterious cyclical poems that appear in what is called "The Pickering Manuscript" after its Victorian owner, B. M. Pickering.

The best clue to the meaning of these three manuscript poems—"The Golden Net," "The Mental Traveller," and "The Crystal Cabinet"—lies in that cyclical structure itself. The poems, probably written about 1803, when Blake was still involved with *The Four Zoas,* concern the deceptive natural cycle to which we enslave ourselves when we submit to the promptings of the natural heart. As both Blake and Marx see, humanity creates and changes nature; we must not passively submit to it. Through the repetition of phrase or incident, Blake in these poems creates striking counterparts to the "mills," the great circles that we have allowed to enclose us within our skulls, within time, and within this physical universe.

"The Golden Net"

In "The Golden Net," a "young Man" feels pity rather than fury at the plight of three maidens whose visionary garments contain an entire history of repression:

> The one was Cloth'd in flames of fire,
> The other Cloth'd in iron wire,
> The other Cloth'd in tears & sighs. (*CW,* 424)

Desire ("fire") and its restraint ("iron wire") will result in "tears & sighs" unless an apocalyptic solution is offered. The young man has none and is, as a result, enslaved himself by virtue of the pity that the natural heart within him has felt. The maidens spread a net over him:

> Underneath the Net I stray,
> Now entreating Burning Fire,
> Now entreating Iron Wire,
> Now entreating Tears & Sighs. (*CW,* 424)

The repetitions enforce the point, underlining the presence of the cyclical trap. "O when will the morning rise?" the young man wonders; but he has himself insured that the morning of vision and revolution remains far off.

"The Mental Traveller"

The most challenging of the cyclic poems is the difficult "The Mental Traveller," in which the repetitions seem to be the most mocking. The speaker of the poem is a "mental traveller" who will offer a visionary account of life in our fallen world, the world of Generation ("A Land of Men & Women too"). We are told how Nature—Tirzah in Blake's myth—repeats the binding of Orc in every human life, dictating the acceptance of the suffering within nature that Jesus knew at the crucifixion and forming in the process the suffering natural heart:

> She binds iron thorns upon his head,
> She pierces both his hands & feet,
> She cuts his heart out at his side
> To make it feel both cold & heat. (*CW,* 425)

It is this heart that leads human beings first to sexual love and then to the practice of the fallen virtue of pity, a virtue only possible when we *accept* an inadequate world. Pity is often institutionalized into charitable organizations:

> An aged Shadow, soon he fades,
> Wand'ring round an Earthly Cot,
> Full filled all with gems & gold
> Which he by industry had got.
>
> And these are the gems of the Human Soul,
> The rubies & pearls of a lovesick eye,
> The countless gold of the akeing heart,
> The martyr's groan & the lover's sigh.
>
> They are his meat, they are his drink;
> He feeds the Beggar & the Poor

And the wayfaring Traveller:
For ever open is his door. (*CW,* 425)

In the same way that political liberalism is based on an acceptance of capitalism as "natural," liberal institutions such as this elderly man embodies are based on an acceptance of the world as it appears. The ideological foundations of such philanthropy cannot endure the birth of a new concept such as that represented by "A little Female Babe":

And she is all of solid fire
And gems & gold, that none his hand
Dares stretch to touch her Baby form,
Or wrap her in his swaddling-band. (*CW,* 425)

The infant Orc, victim of Nature, has turned into the ancient Urizen: he is no longer a creative "male" who can recognize the revolutionary "female" creation that should be the result of his own effort to change the world but instead frightens him. In the world of Generation—the world of separate subject and object, characterized by the existence of the sexes—"male" and "female" are in perpetual conflict, as Los and Enitharmon have already shown in the mythic works.

The reaction that the Urizenic figure brings into being, an analogue to political reaction, destroys even the charitable institutions to leave us face to face with the desert of ratio perception:

The Senses roll themselves in fear,
And the flat Earth becomes a Ball;

The stars, sun, Moon, all shrink away,
A desart vast without a bound.
And nothing left to eat or drink,
And a dark desart all around. (*CW,* 426)

Yet, on the other hand, a new idea has come into being that has in fact jolted the male figure out of his liberalism and into a conservatism that is unacceptable for the continuation of human life ("nothing left to eat or drink"). The Urizenic figure thus casts off his ideological baggage to become rapidly more youthful until he is again the infant Orc who is not yet victim to the ancient abstraction "Nature":

> he becomes a wayward Babe,
> And she a weeping Woman Old.
> Then many a Lover wanders here;
> The Sun & Stars are nearer roll'd. (*CW,* 426)

The world becomes momentarily more human as lovers walk in free-dom again and as the stars cease to be quite as remote as they usually are. But, because the "female" is restrictive nature again, reaction is inevitable:

> They cry "The Babe! the Babe is Born!"
> And flee away on Every side.
>
> For who dare touch the frowning form,
> His arm is wither'd to its root;
> Lions, Boars, Wolves, all howling flee,
> And every Tree does shed its fruit.
>
> And none can touch that frowning form,
> Except it be a Woman Old;
> She nails him down upon the Rock,
> And all is done as I have told. (*CW,* 427)

No hope of human satisfaction—or of a human life at all—is possible if one continues to accept "nature" as both given and determining. Political change is a source of hope only when it is based on a philosophic under-standing that permits an active intervention into that world that seems fixed. If political faiths are based on an acceptance of nature as given in the natural cycles, and therefore also based on an acceptance through empiri-cal epistemology of both a commodified world and a commodified human-ity, they too will fail. Our happiness is to be found only when we can shatter all the enclosing wheels of nature and history, put an end to alien-ation and the division of labor, and establish a fully human existence.

As William Adams has very well explained, in the future that Marx envisions after the end of private property, "The eye has become a *human* eye, just as its *object* has become a social, *human* object, made by man for man."[1] Blake would make the same projection, calling this life Eternity, as experienced by our Divine Humanity.

"The Crystal Cabinet"

If "The Mental Traveller" offers hints about the impossibility of success in political endeavor that is based on an acceptance of the world as it is currently constituted, "The Crystal Cabinet" offers a clear warning against a reliance on sexuality to lead to transcendence of our condition. In this poem, the speaker encounters a maiden who seems to be able to offer him entry into a realm that is, somehow, this physical world repeated in a finer tone:

> She put me into her Cabinet
> And Lock'd me up with a golden Key.
>
> The Cabinet is form'd of Gold
> And Pearl & Crystal shining bright,
> And within it opens into a World
> And a little lovely Moony Night.
>
> Another England there I saw,
> Another London with its Tower,
> Another Thames & other Hills,
> And another pleasant Surrey Bower. (*CW,* 429)

If he could possess her here, he might possess a Keatsian—or Lawrentian—eternity:

> like a flame I burn'd;
> I bent to Kiss the lovely Maid,
> And found a Threefold Kiss return'd. (*CW,* 429)

But his attempt must fail, and his actual subservience to nature is instead emphasized:

I strove to seize the inmost Form
With ardor fierce & hands of flame,
But burst the Crystal Cabinet,
And like a Weeping Babe became—

A weeping Babe upon the wild,
And Weeping Woman pale reclin'd,
And in the outward air again
I fill'd with woes the passing Wind. (*CW,* 429–30)

Nature is to be destroyed or transcended. Its "inmost Form," could it be grasped, provides only the grounds for the despair of the empiricist. If we do not strive for change that is fundamental and grounded in a philosophy and theology that breaks with the empiricists, neither politics nor sexual love hold out hope for the satisfaction of human needs.

These three cyclical poems offer a particularly effective statement against trusting either political reformism or indeed a sexual "revolution," such as we were said to have experienced in the 1960s, as a final answer. Blake was, like Marx, a thoroughgoing revolutionary in his quest for an end to human alienation, and for Blake that goal meant pressing onto the full freedom of Eternity. "Many persons, such as Paine & Voltaire, with some of the Ancient Greeks, say: 'we will not converse concerning Good & Evil; we will live in Paradise & Liberty.' You may do so in Spirit, but not in the Mortal Body as you pretend, till after the Last Judgment" (*CW,* 615–16). (It is worth recalling here Blake's explanation of how the Last Judgment occurs: "Whenever an Individual rejects Error & Embraces Truth, a Last Judgment passes upon that Individual" [*CW,* 613].) The trap that Paine or Voltaire creates in accepting nature is reproduced in the structure of these poems: nature's seasons or the alternations of revolution and counterrevolution enclose us, as do the tight patterns of repeated incident and repeated phrase. The three cyclical poems, taken together with the other manuscript poems, remind us that, even though Blake chose to devote much of his career to works on a larger scale, he had few peers in the fusion of form and meaning in the short poem.

Chapter Ten

Milton

In *Milton* (c. 1810), Blake returns to his quarrel with the last major epic poet in English. As Blake told us in *The Marriage of Heaven and Hell,* Milton, despite his own energy and imagination, chose to picture a rational and bloodless Jesus. But, if we are to be restored to Eternity, emotion and inspiration must be returned to their rightful place in both art and religion. If Blake's *Jerusalem* is concerned with the English church's turning from accusation to forgiveness of sin, his *Milton* argues for that church's return to prophecy and imagination. Thus Blake's Preface pleads that "the Daughters of Memory shall become the Daughters of Inspiration."

To this end, the rational Greek and Roman thinkers must no longer be set up against "the Sublime of the Bible," an attitude with which the Milton of *Paradise Regained* concurred. We must instead, as artists and Christians, be "just & true to our own imaginations, those Worlds of Eternity in which we shall live for ever in Jesus our Lord." When this truth is achieved, then Jerusalem, the art and religion—the "emanation"—of Albion can be restored to a land now dominated by the "mills" of Newtonian thought. Blake's magnificent lyric, now usually entitled "Jerusalem," completes the Preface:

And did those feet in ancient time
Walk upon England's mountains green?
And was the holy Lamb of God
On England's pleasant pastures seen?

And did the Countenance Divine
Shine forth upon our clouded hills?
And was Jerusalem builded here
Among these dark satanic Mills?

Bring me my Bow of burning gold:
Bring me my Arrows of desire:
Bring me my Spear: O clouds unfold!
Bring me my Chariot of fire.

I will not cease from Mental Fight
Nor shall my Sword sleep in my hand
Till we have built Jerusalem
In England's green & pleasant Land. (*CW,* 480–81)

This poem has long been a "hymn" of the British Labour Party, but it is just as appropriately a hymn of the Church of England. It is Blake's call for a restored, non-"natural" theology based not on Lockean rationality but on a dialectical relationship between subject and object. Once, before the process of alienation began, the Divine Humanity and Jerusalem were a unity. Now most of us have retreated into a sterile subjectivity and inhabit a hostile, separated world composed of the Newtonian "Mills" that scientists tell us describe the universe. At this early point in the industrial revolution, Blake's reference is to such mental "Mills," but he seems accurately to forecast that scientists of this kind would also provide the technological foundations for the "dark satanic Mills" of British industry. "Would to God," Blake pleads, rather than there be such scientists as these, "that all the Lord's people were prophets."

"Book the First"

Because he was a prophet to the English, Milton must share much of the blame for the current state of English theology with the archvillains— Bacon, Newton, and Locke. *Milton* recounts, therefore, that poet's own return to imagination, his joining Blake in opposition to the Daughters of Memory—mere rationality—and the concomitant ratio perception:

Daughters of Beulah! Muses who inspire the Poet's Song,
Record the journey of immortal Milton thro' your Realms
Of terror & mild moony lustre in soft sexual delusions
Of varied beauty, to delight the wanderer and repose
His burning thirst & freezing hunger! Come into my hand,

By your mild power descending down the Nerves of my right arm
From out the Portals of my brain, where by your ministry
The Eternal Great Humanity Divine planted his Paradise,
And in it caus'd the Spectres of the Dead to take sweet forms
In likeness of himself. Tell also of the False Tongue! vegetated
Beneath your land of shadows, of its sacrifices and
Its offerings: even till Jesus, the image of the Invisible God,
Became its prey, a curse, an offering and an atonement
For Death Eternal in the heavens of Albion & before the Gates
Of Jerusalem his Emanation, in the heavens beneath Beulah.
(*CW,* 481)

Milton's penitential passage through Beulah, the realm where emanations rest from the Intellectual Wars of Eternity, and hence the realm where the events of any myth "exist," is simply his entry into a world created by an artist tied to Generation. (All fallen art is "sexual delusion," but such an identification is not really harsh criticism of it. We shall at last transcend both the sexes and, in art, the need for media extracted from an alien world; but, until then, we welcome "sexual delusion" not as a refuge from Eternity but as a genuine improvement over the anguish of life in Generation.) The degeneration of Christianity into natural religion, with its Druid "sacrifices" and with a Jesus subject to the law in an "atonement," is among Blake's other subjects in this poem. Blake himself writes from the dictation of "The Eternal Great Humanity Divine," which, thanks to the Daughters of Inspiration, is easily accessible in the minds of all the Lord's people.

Milton has of course passed to Eternity as one of "the Elect," as the Calvinist sects would say; but Blake can imagine what Milton's response to the authentic art of Eternity would have to be. He would necessarily receive the sort of instruction in vision that each of Blake's plates is intended to provide. Thus, Milton's errors are revealed to him by his hearing in Eternity "A Bard's Prophetic Song," a Blakean visionary epic in miniature. Indeed, the Bard's song offers a capsule version of *The Book of Urizen* in its description of the creation of the fallen forms of humanity (*CW,* 482–83). But, although that fundamental error in perception is the source of all our woes, Blake's special emphasis for the instruction of the vision of John Milton must be the usurpation of the role of inspiration by reason.

Thus, the Bard's song recounts how Satan, "Newton's Pantocrator, weaving the woof of Locke," gained the use of the "fiery Harrow" of art and religion from Palamabron, who is a true artist and, like Los, is often identified with Blake himself. This story is based on the same tragic confusion about human powers of which, Blake would say, *Paradise Lost* offers the "history." Once Milton hears the events, told in the clear outlines of mythic art, he will be compelled to cast off error: thus the Bard can well say to him, "Mark well my words! they are of your eternal salvation" (*CW,* 482).

The Satan of the Bard's song is not only a fallen Urizen, the embodiment of ratio perception and Law, but also the most admired type of person in the systems that are born of such perception. Thus, when Los is compelled as usual to fix the changes of Urizen, he is also driven to create three classes of humanity that are called by Urizenic religion the Elect, the Redeemed, and the Reprobate. The Elect are those who benefit from "Offering & Atonement in the cruelties of Moral Law" and who, like Satan, depend on the accusation of sin and are exalted in a religion of Druid sacrifices such as Blake felt natural religion to be. The other two classes are the Redeemed, who are seen in Blake's work as those like ourselves, seeking redemption, and the Reprobate, whom the religious might consider to be devils but who are actually the fiery prophets whom we repress both in our society and in our own personalities.

Lambeth, seat of the Church of England, lies metaphorically in ruins and is now a source of the "Oak Groves" and "Druid Temples" of natural religion:

> Lambeth's Vale
> Where Jerusalem's foundations began, where they were laid in ruins,
> Where they were laid in ruins from every Nation, & Oak Groves rooted,
> Dark gleams before the Furnace-mouth a heap of burning ashes.
> When shall Jerusalem return & overspread all the Nations?
> Return, return to Lambeth's Vale, O building of human souls!
> Thence stony Druid Temples overspread the Island white,
> And thence from Jerusalem's ruins, from her walls of salvation
> And praise, thro' the whole Earth were rear'd. (*CW,* 485–86)

From what was once, and will again be, the foundation of Jerusalem in England, faulty perception based on faulty psychology spreads its cancer.

Satan interferes with the harrow of art, just as the church has allowed ratio perception to intrude upon inspiration. He cannot manage it, of course, just as rational inquiries into Christianity bring only despair. And similarly Palamabron cannot keep the sober order that Satan's mills require:

> Los beheld
> The servants of the Mills drunken with wine and dancing wild
> With shouts and Palamabron's songs, rending the forests green
> With ecchoing confusion. (*CW,* 488)

In the contention that follows, Theotormon and Bromion, familiar as the mistaken accusers of sin in *Visions of the Daughters of Albion,* support Satan. Rintrah, by contrast, the wrathful prophet of *The Marriage of Heaven and Hell,* opposes him.

An assembly is called to judge; but, as happened in Milton's bifurcation of Jesus into two men, one rational and one energetic, and in the church's drift toward natural religion, the blame falls—quite unfairly—on the prophet Rintrah. With this result, Satan is free to denounce Palamabron, to promulgate his moral laws, and to assert his dominance: "'I am God alone: / There is no other! let all obey my principles of moral individuality'" (*CW,* 490). Historically, and perhaps in part because of the prophet Milton, Christians now "worship Satan under the Unutterable Name." Within our civilization, Satan's victory is best seen in the depression of art and inspiration and in the dominance of natural religion. The doctrine of atonement replaces the forgiveness of sins: "one must die for another throughout all Eternity" (*CW,* 491).

Leutha, "a Daughter of Beulah" but frequently associated with feelings of guilt as in *Visions of the Daughters of Albion,* recognizes Satan's error and tries to take the blame for it herself. She sees Satan's crime as a longing for the life of art inspired by her own love for Palamabron, but such confusion of roles is possible only because of an earlier fall: "The Sin was begun in Eternity and will not rest to Eternity." Despite her plea, the stonification of the world is finished; the prophets become the Reprobate: Jesus Himself "died as a Reprobate, he was Punish'd as a Transgressor" (*CW,* 494). British theology sinks into the mire of empiricism: "In dreams [Leutha] bore Rahab, the mother of Tirzah, & her sisters / In Lambeth's vales, in Cambridge & in Oxford, places of Thought." And here the Bard, who has sung "According to the inspiration of the Poetic Genius / Who is the eternal all-protecting Divine Humanity," ends his song.

The Bard enters Milton's bosom, indicating thereby his having achieved total communication with him. Milton immediately realizes that he has been mistaken to wear "the robe of the promise" as one of the Elect. He will return to life ("Eternal Death") to try to bring an end to the errors he once helped gain a footing in England. He will try to restore his emanation to himself, an emanation that is now as separate from him, he realizes, as Jerusalem is from Albion. He realizes that he has shared the solipsism of empirical perception, creating a hermaphroditic form for humanity: "he beheld his own Shadow / A mournful form double, hermaphroditic, male & female / In one wonderful body" (*CW,* 496). Thus Milton returns to earth, entering Blake's left foot.

As Milton returns to corporeal life, his real body, the spiritual one, remains in Eternity. Thus, it is only Milton's shadow that will walk again on Earth. (Because objectification of "self" or "body" breaks the unity of subject and object, it is only the shadow of any human being's eternal individuality that leads one's corporeal life.) He passes the vortices of other universes, perceiving them as spheres because he is not within them; but he does enter the vortex of Earth, which he can perceive as it is, as the "one infinite plain" that the perception of every human shows it to be. (Thus Blake would assert that the earth was flat.) Milton locates his biographical emanation, his three wives and three daughters who are locked in Ulro and are frozen abstractions rather than the dynamic participants in Jerusalem that they might be. Still ready to take dictation, they surround him; and they ask that he be their Moses, his body the "Rock Sinai" from which he will promulgate the Puritan vision. But Milton leaves them; instead, he enters the London that Los strives to make visionary but that is bound in the bands of natural religion.

Los is frightened by Milton's appearance, particularly since Enitharmon exults that he has come so that "Satan shall be unloos'd upon Albion." Indeed, the natural world seems to rejoice at Milton's return because it seems it will now be enthroned as the basis for a system of natural religion from which there is no appeal:

And thus the Shadowy Female howls in articulate howlings:
"I will lament over Milton in the lamentations of the afflicted:
My Garments shall be woven of sighs & heart broken lamentations:
The misery of unhappy Families shall be drawn into its border,

Wrought with the needle with dire sufferings, poverty, pain & woe
Along the rocky Island & thence throughout the whole Earth;
There shall be the sick Father & his starving Family, there
The Prisoner in the stone Dungeon & the Slave at the Mill.
I will have writings written all over it in Human Words
That every Infant that is born upon the Earth shall read
And get by rote as a hard task of a life of sixty years.
I will have Kings inwoven upon it & Councellors & Mighty Men:
The Famine shall clasp it together with buckles & Clasps,
And the Pestilence shall be its fringe & the War its girdle
To divide into Rahab & Tirzah that Milton may come to our tents.
For I will put on the Human Form & take the Image of God,
Even Pity & Humanity, but my Clothing shall be Cruelty:
And I will put on Holiness as a breastplate & as a helmet,
And all my ornaments shall be of the gold of broken hearts,
And the precious stones of anxiety & care & desperation & death
And repentance for sin & sorrow & punishment & fear,
To defend me from thy terrors, O Orc, my only beloved!" (*CW,* 499)

Virtues of the natural heart will replace real humanity, and "Holiness"
will be entirely allied with warfare. All that is energetic and imaginative
will be repressed through conceptions of "sin," and the young will "read
/ And get by rote" an ideology that assures their own oppression. Orc
tries to resist, but his efforts only lead to the appearance of Urizen, who
is as stony and as icy as ever.

But Milton's return has not been understood. He has heard the Bard's
song, he has realized that the Puritan Milton was "Satan," and a new
Milton has been born who counters Urizen's attempt to inflict the icy
baptism of rationality on his head:

> with cold hand Urizen stoop'd down
> And took up water from the river Jordan, pouring on
> To Milton's brain the icy fluid from his broad cold palm.
> But Milton took of the red clay of Succoth, moulding it with care
> Between his palms and filling up the furrows of many years,
> Beginning at the feet of Urizen, and on the bones

Creating new flesh on the Demon cold and building him
As with new clay, a Human form in the Valley of Beth Peor.
(*CW,* 500)

Milton will force Urizen to be human rather than allow his own
achieved humanity to be Urizenic again. Since Succoth is the place to
which Jesus went after the Crucifixion, Milton is trying to shape Urizen
into the resurrected Humanity. Milton's emanations, aspects of the emanation of the Puritan Milton, are traitors to the cause of the imagination;
but they have already been identified as Rahab and Tirzah, natural religion and delusive nature, who sing the praises of natural religion, offer
to sacrifice Jerusalem, and assert the superiority of nature to Jesus:

Where is the Lamb of God? where is the promise of his coming?
Her shadowy Sisters form the bones, even the bones of Horeb
Around the marrow, and the orbed scull around the brain.
His images are born for War, for Sacrifice to Tirzah,
To Natural Religion, to Tirzah, the Daughter of Rahab the Holy!
(*CW,* 501)

They offer Milton the position to which he in some sense aspired in setting out to be England's great epic poet: they offer him the kingship of
"Canaan," a false promised land woven of rationality and nature; but
Milton now serves only Albion, who begins to awaken.
    Milton knows now how to view the seemingly frozen natural world
that our bad perception gives us. He knows, as does Blake, that "the little winged fly . . . has a heart like thee, a brain open to heaven and hell"
and that all that alien world of fierce animals and cold stone is human.
He would now say with Blake:

Seek not the heavenly father then beyond the skies,
There Chaos dwells & ancient Night & Og & Anak old.
For every human heart has gates of brass & bars of adamant
Which few dare unbar, because dread Og & Anak guard the gates
Terrific: and each mortal brain is wall'd and moated round
Within, and Og & Anak watch here: here is the Seat

Of Satan in its Webs: for in brain and heart and loins
Gates open beneath Satan's Seat to the City of Golgonooza,
Which is the spiritual fourfold London in the loins of Albion.
(*CW,* 302)

Indeed, since Milton has entered Blake's foot, his restored vision is one
with Blake's. Blake sees the world as totally humanized, as a mere sandal for that visionary foot: "all this Vegetable World appear'd on my left
Foot / As a bright sandal form'd immortal." And the imaginative Milton
will soon be reunited with his proper emanation, Ololon, who represents
what might have been had Milton's theology not been tainted with
rationality and the law. Ololon, uniting with Jesus and thus representing
a restored theology, prepares to descend to be reunited with Milton.

Not only does Milton combine with Blake, but Los does too. The
union occurs in Lambeth, where Jerusalem's foundations once were and
where they will again be if natural theology can be overcome. Rintrah
and Palamabron, sons of Los, at first fear Milton because they understand that he has contributed significantly to the establishment of the
erroneous views of the natural theologian:

And all the Daughters of Los prophetic wail; yet in deceit
They weave a new Religion from the new jealousy of Theotormon.
Milton's Religion is the cause: there is no end to destruction.
Seeing the Churches at their Period in terror & despair,
Rahab created Voltaire, Tirzah created Rousseau,
Asserting the Self-righteousness against the Universal Saviour,
Mocking the Confessors & Martyrs, claiming Self-righteousness,
With cruel Virtue making War upon the Lamb's Redeemed
To perpetuate War & Glory, to perpetuate the Laws of Sin.
They perverted Swedenborg's Visions in Beulah & in Ulro
To destroy Jerusalem as a Harlot & her Sons as Reprobates,
To raise up Mystery the Virgin Harlot, Mother of War,
Babylon the Great, the Abomination of Desolation. (*CW,* 506)

They do know that the Evangelical movement has provided hints of a
return to imaginative religion:

But then I rais'd up Whitefield, Palamabron rais'd up Westley,
And these are the cries of the Churches before the two Witnesses.
Faith in God the dear Saviour who took on the likeness of men,
Becoming obedient to death, even the death of the Cross.
The Witnesses lie dead in the Street of the Great City:
No Faith is in all the Earth: the Book of God is trodden under Foot.
He sent his two Servants, Whitefield & Westley: were they Prophets,
Or were they Idiots or Madmen? shew us miracles!
Can you have greater Miracles than these? Men who devote
Their life's whole comfort to intire scorn & injury & death?
Awake, thou sleeper on the Rock of Eternity! Albion awake!
(*CW,* 506)

But Rintrab and Palamabron do not recognize that Milton now aids
rather than hinders the work begun by the Evangelicals. Los pleads for a
kind of ecumenism that would include Milton too: "Remember how
Calvin and Luther in fury premature / Sow'd War and stern division
between Papists & Protestants. / Let it not be so now! O go not forth in
Martyrdoms & Wars!" (*CW,* 507). Los remains "The Watchman of
Eternity," the inspired prophet; and he can see Milton as "the Signal that
the Last Vintage now approaches."

The restoration of humanity can begin now that Milton is free from
the shackles of natural religion. Blake's concern in what remains of
"Book the First" of *Milton* is to demonstrate what "nature" really is. All
the particles of the created world will be crushed in the "Wine-press" of
vision when we tear to bits the frozen Urizenic world that we had
thought it necessary to inhabit. Change will begin in Lambeth with the
expulsion of natural religion from the church:

you shall Reap the whole Earth from Pole to Pole, from Sea to Sea,
Beginning at Jerusalem's Inner Court, Lambeth, ruin'd and given
To the detestable Gods of Priam, to Apollo, and at the Asylum
Given to Hercules, who labour in Tirzah's Looms for bread,
Who set Pleasure against Duty, who Create Olympic crowns
To make Learning a burden & the Work of the Holy Spirit, Strife:
The Thor & cruel Odin who first rear'd the Polar Caves.

Lambeth mourns, calling Jerusalem: she weeps & looks abroad
For the Lord's coming, that Jerusalem may overspread all Nations.
(*CW,* 511)

We can tear apart the physical world, or do with it what we will, when
we come to see it as what it is—fully a product of the imagination. Thus
everything we perceive is born of Los:

These are the Children of Los; thou seest the Trees on mountains,
The wind blows heavy, loud they thunder thro' the darksom sky,
Uttering prophecies & speaking instructive words to the sons
Of men: These are the Sons of Los: These the Visions of Eternity,
But we see only as it were the hem of their garments
When with our vegetable eyes we view these wondrous Visions.
(*CW,* 512)

Ratio perception has closed these worlds of delight, but they can be
opened again.

Similarly, the barriers seemingly provided by time are only creations
of Los. For the prophet, there has always been human time to break
through the sequence of hours:

Every Time less than a pulsation of the artery
Is equal in its period & value to Six Thousand Years,
For in this Period the Poet's Work is Done, and all the Great
Events of Time start forth & are conciev'd in such a Period,
Within a Moment, a Pulsation of the Artery. (*CW,* 516)

In any case, what we call Time is a special gift from Los; it is "the mercy
of Eternity" because it is, in fact, speeding toward apocalypse.

The so-called "Science" of a Newton, on which natural religion was
built, is replaced on these last few plates of "Book the First" of *Milton* by
"the Science of the Elohim," which makes it evident that everything is
holy. Blake asserts that "every Natural Effect has a Spiritual Cause . . .
for a Natural Cause only seems" (*CW,* 513). He mocks the "Microscope"
and the "Telescope" (as he did in the case of the superempiricist
Bromion) because they only "alter / The ratio of the Spectator's Organs."
In truth:

> every Space larger than a red Globule of Man's blood
> Is visionary, and is created by the Hammer of Los:
> And every Space smaller than a Globule of Man's blood opens
> Into Eternity of which this vegetable Earth is but a shadow.
> (*CW,* 516)

Infinity awaits us in either direction, as every twentieth-century scientist knows.

With the improved epistemology of Milton, natural religion is robbed of one of its pillars, the belief in "nature." The church can begin to be reborn in Lambeth, and this vegetable world can cease to screen off Eternity. If Milton can now embrace his proper emanation—he has rejected all that was mistaken—Jerusalem can analogously be restored to Albion. Then "all the Lord's people" can be "Prophets."

"Book the Second"

In "Book the Second," Ololon, Milton's true emanation and therefore a sound art and theology, descends into Beulah, the usual refuge for emanations. And because Beulah, land of inspiration, does "terminate in rocky Albion," because even the stony world of Generation has art as a window onto the truth, the residents of "all Nations" can now see "the Lord coming / In the clouds of Ololon with Power & Great Glory." "War"—that is "Not Mental, as the Wars of Eternity"—dominates fallen humankind; but the lamentation of Beulah over Ololon, who is still not restored to Milton, challenges men with inspired beauty, as does the song of birds or the odor of flowers: the sense of what is missing in our lives is spreading, and "Men are sick with Love."

Milton no longer has any sympathy for "The Idiot Reasoner" who "laughs at the Man of Imagination." His immortal part, still in Eternity as is the visionary part of each of us, hears the instruction of "the Seven Angels of the Presence," who warn against Satan and against judging individuals rather than the states that they are in. But "The Imagination is not a State: it is the Human Existence itself." We hear the divine vision calling for the restoration of Jerusalem, whose place in Albion has been usurped by Babylon, and we are instructed in the levels of "Humanity in its Repose"—beneath dynamic Eternity—which are called Beulah, Alla, Al-Ulro, and Or-Ulro, a systemization of the levels of vision not found in this precise form elsewhere in Blake.

After all this information has been imparted—all of it imaginative and valuable—Ololon has even more cause to lament the world humans now inhabit, for it is "a frozen bulk subject to decay & death" (*CW,* 525). Perhaps our situation appears to the Eternals even worse than it really is since, not having undergone incarnation, they do not see the hope that is created even by the Generation-bound artist:

> they
> Could not behold Golgonooza without passing the Polypus,
> A wondrous journey not passable by Immortal feet, & none
> But the Divine Saviour can pass it without annihilation.
> For Golgonooza cannot be seen till having pass'd the Polypus
> It is viewed on all sides round by a Four-fold Vision,
> Or till you become Mortal & Vegetable in Sexuality,
> Then you behold its mighty Spires & Domes of ivory & gold.
> (*CW,* 525)

But Ololon will, as Milton did earlier, risk annihilation to descend to earth. She finds one of the gaps in time that we have considered before:

> There is a Moment in each Day that Satan cannot find,
> Nor can his Watch Fiends find it; but the Industrious find
> This Moment & it multiply, & when it once is found
> It renovates every Moment of the Day if rightly placed.
> In this moment Ololon descended to Los & Enitharmon. (*CW,* 526)

Ololon, who had been "multitudes" before, can now, having entered the Polypus, be seen as "A Virgin of twelve years." She appears to Blake in Felpham, the location of the cottage in which he worked as an artist "To display Nature's cruel holiness, the deceits of Natural Religion."

Ololon will be Milton's emanation, so now, to complete the usual division of an individual in Blake's system, we get a full vision of Milton's Spectre (*CW,* 527–30). This spectre, a compound of all forms of natural religion, is the Covering Cherub that keeps us from Paradise. Ultimately, he is that Satan who has bound "Jerusalem . . . in chains in the Dens of Babylon." Milton knows that Satan is his Spectre (*CW,* 529) and is ready to cast off all that belongs to the "Natural Heart." Satan resists and asks deification as "God the judge of all." With this stark opposition, the tension has reached a breaking point. Albion, England, is reanimated, and the giant figure Albion walks, gaining particular support from the cathedral cities:

> London & Bath & Legions & Edinburgh
> Are the four pillars of his Throne: his left foot near London
> Covers the shades of Tyburn: his instep from Windsor
> To Primrose Hill stretching to Highgate & Holloway.
> London is between his knees, its basements fourfold;
> His right foot stretches to the sea on Dover cliffs, his heel
> On Canterbury's ruins; his right hand covers lofty Wales,
> His left Scotland; his bosom girt with gold involves
> York, Edinburgh, Durham & Carlisle, & on the front
> Bath, Oxford, Cambridge, Norwich; his right elbow
> Leans on the Rocks of Erin's Land, Ireland, ancient nation.
> His head bends over London. (*CW,* 531)

Ololon feels that she cannot face the full embodiment of error that the times have wrought: "this thing, this Newtonian Phantasm, / This Voltaire & Rousseau, this Hume & Gibbon & Bolingbroke, / This Natural Religion, this impossible absurdity" (*CW,* 532).

But Milton's total espousal of the imaginative leads to the statement that is ultimately to console Ololon, destroy Satan, and restore Jerusalem to Albion:

> "I come in Self-annihilation & the grandeur of Inspiration,
> To cast off Rational Demonstration by Faith in the Saviour,
> To cast off the rotten rags of Memory by Inspiration,
> To cast off Bacon, Locke & Newton from Albion's covering,
> To take off his filthy garments & clothe him with Imagination,
> To cast aside from Poetry all that is not Inspiration,
> That it no longer shall dare to mock with the aspersion of Madness
> Cast on the Inspired by the tame high finisher of paltry Blots
> Indefinite, or paltry Rhymes, or paltry Harmonies,
> Who creeps into State Government like a catterpiller to destroy;

To cast off the idiot Questioner who is always questioning
But never capable of answering, who sits with a sly grin
Silent plotting when to question, like a thief in a cave,
Who publishes doubt & calls it knowledge, whose Science is Despair,
Whose pretence to knowledge is envy, whose whole Science is
To destroy the wisdom of ages to gratify ravenous Envy
That rages round him like a Wolf day & night without rest:
He smiles with condescension, he talks of Benevolence & Virtue,
And those who act with Benevolence & Virtue they murder time on time.
These are the destroyers of Jerusalem, these are the murderers
Of Jesus, who deny the Faith & mock at Eternal Life,
Who pretend to Poetry that they may destroy Imagination
By imitation of Nature's Images drawn from Remembrance.
These are the Sexual Garments, the Abomination of Desolation,
Hiding the Human Lineaments as with an Ark & Curtains
Which Jesus rent & now shall wholly purge away with Fire
Till Generation is swallowed up in Regeneration." (*CW*, 533)

The full Blakean faith is in these lines which begin with the replacement of the Daughters of Memory by the Daughters of Inspiration and which move to a restored Jerusalem and to Jesus' triumph over nature.

Ololon enters the breast of the Milton who now speaks fully from inspiration. The world is ready for apocalypse: "clouds roll over London with a south wind; soft Oothcon Pants in the Vales of Lambeth, weeping o'er her Human Harvest" (*CW*, 535). Oothoon, the spirit of America and thus as representative of Liberty as is Jerusalem, is returned to Lambeth. The wine presses will begin their work of restoring the frozen particles of our world to visionary ones. "Terrific Lions & Tygers" seem bursting with the portions of Eternity that they contain. And here, abruptly, Blake's *Milton* ends: poised on the verge of the final return to Eternity. If we have been attentive readers, our minds are expanded to the bursting point; and, with our "faculties roused to act," we may take the next step into Eternity on our own.

Leaning against the pillars. & his disease rose from his skirts
Upon the Precipice he stood:ready to fall into Non-Entity.

Los was all astonishment & terror: he trembled sitting on the Stone
Of London: but the interiors of Albions fibres & nerves were hidden
From Los; astonished he beheld only the petrified surfaces,
And saw his Furnaces in ruins. for Los is the Demon of the Furnaces;
He saw also the Four Points of Albion reversd inwards
He siezd his Hammer & Tongs, his iron Poker & his Bellows,
Upon the valleys of Middlesex. Shouting loud for aid Divine.

In stern defiance came from Albions bosom. Hand, Hyle, Koban,
Gwantok, Peachy. Brertun, Slaid. Hutln. Skofeld. Kock. Kotope
Bowen. Albions Sons: they bore him a golden couch into the porch
And on the Couch reposd his limbs, trembling from the bloody field.
Rearing their Druid Patriarchal rocky Temples around his limbs.
All things begin & end. in Albions Ancient Druid Rocky Shore.)

By permission of the Houghton Library, Harvard University.

Chapter Eleven

Jerusalem

Chapter 1

Blake's *Jerusalem* (c. 1820) recounts the passage of the human consciousness from what we call life ("Eternal Death" to Blake) to authentic life in
Eternity. Blake himself writes with "Enthusiasm," accepting the inspiration of Jesus, the human imagination: "I see the Saviour over me /
Spreading his beams of love & dictating the words of this mild song"
(*CW*, 622). "Mild" may seem the wrong word for an epic poem filled
with anguished incident, but it is right for Blake since his vision will
transcend this world of chaos and war to restore us to Eternity.[1]

Unlike Blake, however, at the poem's beginning Albion turns from
the Jesus who assures him that "I am not a God afar off . . . Within your
bosoms I reside, and you reside in me." Albion, showing fully the mental habits of one controlled by Urizen, rejects Jerusalem, the imaginative
realm that he should inhabit, to say "by demonstration man alone can
live" and plans to "build . . . Laws of Moral Virtue" in opposition to "The
Spirit of Jesus," which is "continual forgiveness of Sin." Thus, Albion is
like Urizen "in jealous fears . . . darkening, cold"; and the world that
could be humanized is frozen into the alien shapes of the world that we
inhabit: "every Human perfection / Of mountain & river & city are small
& wither'd & darken'd."

Blake labors in this poem to resurrect this world to its true humanity
through the restoration of Jerusalem to Albion. To accomplish this resurrection, he needs "to open the immortal eyes / Of Man inwards into
the Worlds of Thought, into Eternity / Ever expanding in the Bosom of
God, the Human Imagination" (*CW*, 623). What he finds at present is
that:

> all within is open'd into the deeps of Entuthon Benython,
> A dark and unknown night, indefinite, unmeasurable, without end,
> Abstract Philosophy warring in enmity against imagination

(Which is the Divine Body, of the Lord Jesus, blessed for ever).
(*CW,* 624)

The forces at enmity with imagination are represented in our fallen world by men like those Blake here names: Hand (probably Robert Hunt, who wrote the review condemning Blake as an insane artist), Hyle (probably Hayley, Blake's insensitive "patron"), Scofield (the soldier Scolfield, who accused Blake of sedition), and by nine other men. As counterparts, they have 12 female forms "united into Tirzah" and "in Rahab" as the deceptive natural world and as the natural theology to which fallen humanity is drawn. But the worst enemy of all to imagination is within Blake himself, within the Los side of his personality. That enemy is, of course, the Spectre of Urthona, all that restrains imaginative artists in their enthusiasm.

The emanations of the Sons of Albion, who are in aggregate the natural world that we inhabit, offer us the "starry wheels" of the Newtonian universe. It is the sight of these that strikes terror into the heart of every imaginative person: thus, for Los, "his Spectre divided / In terror of those starry wheels." The Spectre tries to turn Los against Albion "by tears, by arguments of science & by terrors"—by the doubts that we all have that cause us to turn away from Jesus to attend to the terrible starry wheels themselves. The Spectre can point to all the scorn with which the Sons of Albion greet the products of the imagination. In addition, he can recount the basic Blakean story of the fall—the restriction of energy within the fallen natural world that is carried out with the approval of Urizen and that ends in "a Law of Sin" such as that by which "Scofield, . . . Kox, Kotop, and Bowen," participants in Blake's trial in Chichester, tried to punish him.

Los calmly hears the Spectre's arguments. He asserts his continuing friendship to Albion and forgives enemies of the imagination: "O point of mutual forgiveness between Enemies! / Birthplace of the Lamb of God incomprehensible" (*CW,* 626). Since even Hand (Hunt) can be overcome, the Spectre poses no real threat ("As thou art now, such was he, O Spectre."), and Los begins the restoration of Albion.

Los first asserts his control of the furnaces that represent the dominance of the "physical" over the energetic, the furnaces in which Luvah is sealed by Vala: "Los [is] the sole, uncontrolled Lord of the Furnaces." Since the imagination ultimately is the origin of the physical world, art can free the physical world from its false restrictions. Thus, with the "furnaces" open to him, Los can undo the work of the Sons of Albion, "for the mighty Hand / Condens'd his Emanations into hard opake substances, / And his infant thoughts & desires into cold dark cliffs of death" (*CW*, 628). Because of the action of "Hand," the conflict of ideas that should be the intellectual war of Eternity has become the military warfare that surrounds us.

But Los will "form the spiritual sword / That lays open the hidden heart" to restore "Enthusiasm and Life," and imaginative art will once again be born from the physical world. To the Spectre, such art is made up of "the Sins / That thou callest thy Children"; and Los's emanation Enitharmon, the sum total of all his works of art, is the "Great Sin." The Spectre has this view of art because his God "is not a Being of Pity and Compassion, / He cannot feel Distress, he feeds on Sacrifice & Offering." Los, however, realizes that his Spectre makes "Holy" the "Reasoning Power, And in its Holiness is closed the Abomination of Desolation." He does not see his artistic creations, the Sons of Los, as sins; instead, he calls them from the furnaces to aid in the restoration of Albion's emanation, Jerusalem.

Los and the Sons of Los labor to turn London into Golgonooza, the city of art that will properly house Jerusalem and so restore her to Albion. Opposed to their activity is that of the Sons of Albion, who are often represented as a group by Hand, who are trying to build Babylon, the home of Vala. The Sons of Los know that Vala should not be embodied since such an embodiment creates "nature" and natural religion; but the Sons of Albion have already granted Vala her independent existence by permitting the separation of their emanations, Tirzah and Rahab, who together are Vala.

Golgonooza (probably "New Golgotha") will have four gates; and at the center are Luban, Los's palace, and the golden looms of Cathedron, where Jerusalem's web of life is woven.[2] A city built "fourfold" in the wisdom of fully imaginative vision, it lets us see that "the Vegetative Universe opens like a flower from the Earth's center / In which is Eternity." This city restores to Albion the reality that experience, as opposed to rationality, holds out for all:

In those Churches ever consuming & ever building by the Spectres
Of all the inhabitants of Earth wailing to be Created,
Shadowy to those who dwell not in them, meer possibilities,
But to those who enter into them they seem the only substances;
For every thing exists & not one sigh nor smile nor tear,
One hair nor particle of dust, not one can pass away. (*CW*, 634)

Golgonooza restores that center of reality and truth that no sane person would deny, except for Locke and Newton: "I turn my eyes to the Schools & Universities of Europe / And there behold the Loom of Locke, whose Woof rages dire, / Wash'd by the Water-wheels of Newton" (*CW,* 636). Golgonooza contains all of England, as Blake is at some pains to show us, and all that humans have done or felt:

> All things acted on Earth are seen in the bright Sculptures of
> Los's Halls, & every Age renews its powers from these Works
> With every pathetic story possible to happen from Hate or
> Wayward Love; & every sorrow & distress is carved here,
> Every Affinity of Parents, Marriages & Friendships are here
> In all their various combinations wrought with wondrous Art,
> All that can happen to Man in his pilgrimage of seventy years.
> Such is the Divine Written Law of Horeb & Sinai, And such the
> Holy Gospel of Mount Olivet & Calvary. (*CW,* 638)

Despite Los's ability to perform the artistic function, he is himself a victim of the imbalance in the faculties of Albion. Thus, no matter what he does to stop it, his emanation Enitharmon separates from him. Even for the visionary artist there is the mundane existence in which the delusions of space and time are operative. At least Los knows that Enitharmon (space) is his emanation, "Piteous image of my soft desires & loves"; and he will seek reunion with her.

Meanwhile, the Sons of Albion see Jerusalem as "a sin and shame" and seek to enthrone Vala in Babylon. In doing this, they turn on the imagination and thereby threaten to "destroy the Divine Saviour." Jerusalem and Vala quarrel in Lambeth, symbolically the seat of the Church of England, over their respective theological positions. Jerusalem is for imagination and the forgiveness of sins ("What is Sin but a little / Error & fault that is soon forgotten?"); Vala is for natural theology and the accusation of sin. And, unfortunately, the deluded Albion intrudes to agree with Vala, sees sin in Jerusalem, and rejects her. His decision brings about state religion, whose result is war: "Why should Punishment Weave the Veil with Iron Wheels of War / When Forgiveness might it Weave with Wings of Cherubim?" Thus he joins his sons in a crime against Jesus: "O Human Imagination, O Divine Body I have Crucified, / I have turned my back upon thee into the Wastes of Moral Law" (*CW,* 647).

Once, Blake tells us, England was the home of Jerusalem, and its real faith spread over the world: "In the Exchanges of Jerusalem every Nation walk'd, / And London walk'd in every Nation, mutual in love & harmony." But now the Sons of Albion build Babylon instead. Only the imaginative remnant that longs for salvation from this world of "Oaken Groves" and "Dragon Temples" pleads: "Descend, O Lamb of God, & take away the imputation of Sin / By the Creation of States & the deliverance of Individuals Evermore. Amen" (*CW,* 648). The destruction of moral categories by forgiveness—forgiveness that "breaks" the Ten Commandments—will remove Vala from Lambeth and allow Golgonooza to replace Babylon. "States" are real categories, but no individual need remain in a state to be punished for a sin.

Chapter 2

Perhaps the most startling assertion made in the latter part of chapter 1 of *Jerusalem,* at least for a reader new to Blake, is that Jerusalem was once in England. Blake resumes this argument again in his epistle "To the Jews" that opens chapter 2. As he asserts, the "inhabitants of Earth" are "united" "in One Religion, The Religion of Jesus." Hence all that surrounds us, whether "England" or "Israel," should be viewed as the emanation of the divine imagination in us and therefore as Jerusalem. Thus, before human alienation began, "In the Exchanges of London every Nation walk'd, / And London walk'd in every Nation." Consequently, it is fair to say that the Jewish patriarchs were "Druids" and that "All things Begin & End in Albion's Ancient Druid Rocky Shore."

After the prose argument, Blake offers all the proof the imagination would need in a lovely companion lyric to that which began *Milton:*

> The fields from Islington to Marybone,
> To Primrose Hill and Saint John's Wood,
>   Were builded over with pillars of gold,
> And there Jerusalem's pillars stood.

To restore Jerusalem to England, the forgiveness of sins must again dominate British Christianity:

Forgiving trespasses and sins
  Lest Babylon with cruel Og
    With Moral & Self-righteous Law
  Should Crucify in Satan's Synagogue! (*CW,* 650)

At present, however, Albion is so enslaved by moral virtue that, as chapter 2 opens, he sits at Tyburn where the gallows stood and where would now be the "deadly tree" of "Moral Virtue and the Law of God who dwells in Chaos hidden from the human sight." But Jesus, the Divine Vision, again appears behind Kensington Gardens "where was mild Zion Hill's / Most ancient promontory." Jesus sees the decay in religion that the Sons of Albion have wrought; for Lambeth,[3] seat of the church, London, and Oxford are victims of natural theology: "The City of the Woods in the Forest of Ephratah is taken! / London is a stone of her ruins, Oxford is the dust of her walls" (*CW,* 653).

Since *Jerusalem* began *in medias res,* an account of how Albion fell is useful at this point. This narrative is provided by Enitharmon and the Spectre of Urthona who "alone . . . escaped" from Albion's fall. We are told that Albion created a Urizenic god "from his wearied intellect" and fell to worship it; and this occurrence is, of course, exactly what has befallen the churches in the grip of natural religion (as the speech of Jesus told us). As a result, the "vast form of Nature like a serpent" denies Luvah and Vala their proper roles, and "All is confusion" (*CW,* 655).

Los holds the escaped Enitharmon and Spectre of Urthona, aspects of fallen art, within him, and he tours the ruins of Jerusalem in London and finally rests on London Stone near Tyburn. He hears the contentions of Jerusalem and Vala: Jerusalem argues for "Faith" against "Demonstration," and Vala maintains that "Urizen is the Champion of Albion." All events seem to support Vala's cause. The Sons of Albion build "Druid . . . Temples," and Albion's Rational Power ("the Great Selfhood, / Satan, Worship'd as God by the Mighty Ones of the Earth") appears to denounce everything that is human. Vala follows up to assert that, in any case, the human form is just another natural form and not a spiritual one ("The Imaginative Human Form is but a breathing of Vala"). In her, the female will (natural law) triumphs:

what may Woman be
  To have power over Man from Cradle to corruptible Grave?
  There is a Throne in every Man, it is the Throne of God;
  This, Woman has claim'd as her own, & Man is no more! (*CW,* 661)

The Divine Humanity has already been denied in Vala's previous assertion that she creates even the human form. From Blake's time forward, "scientific" accounts of humans have been based on the assumptions of the total materialism that she represents.

"Reuben" enters the myth at this point to represent humanity fallen to the level that Vala has defined. He is natural humanity or, as Blake puts it, "vegetative-man"; but "Merlin," who is also present, suggests the possibility of an imaginative remnant among us. Fortunately, humans will fall no lower than Reuben (a sort of Adam) because Jesus has set "the two limits, Satan and Adam," the limits of opacity and contraction; therefore, we will not see a world more stonified than we now see, nor will we see humanity as less than Reuben or Adam. When the divine imagination sets these limits, the act is essentially the same as that of Los who fixed the changes of Urizen; but here the imaginative act is seen from its positive side as an act of mercy.

Our world perceived as "Elements" and as "Length, Bredth & Highth" is formed as it was in *The Book of Urizen*. The Eternals find our moral laws absurd:

> Have you known the judgment that is arisen among the
> Zoas of Albion, where a Man dare hardly to embrace
> His own Wife for the terrors of Chastity that they call
> By the name of Morality? (*CW*, 663)

But Albion keeps his humanity bound in "petrific hardness" and keeps away all that might touch "His hidden heart." Jesus follows him to offer the hope of imaginative vision, while London urges him "let us awake up together," but Albion is unmoved; he is looking for "Atonement," which the law would demand, rather than for mercy. Los points, without effect upon Albion, to the cruel vision of spiritual existence to which Albion chooses to adhere: "Must the Wise die for an Atonement? does Mercy endure Atonement? / No! It is Moral Severity & destroys Mercy in its Victim" (*CW*, 666). All England mourns Albion's mistaken theology, saying "he hath studied the arts / Of unbelief" (*CW*, 667). The cathedral cities of England, the possessors of "A Human Vision! Human Divine, Jesus the Saviour, blessed for ever and ever," yearn for Albion's restoration.

Albion curses his "own affections / And his own beloveds," the potentially visionary aspects of himself that he beholds in Los's furnaces—even within art that must use a fallen world and that demands "righteousness

& justice." But Los refuses to let Albion destroy "these little ones," his emotions; and he asserts that he himself can, as a visionary, "break [Albion's] bonds of righteousness." Los also indicates that, although we can fall no lower than Adam and nature, we can, when our imagination is freed, expand to infinity: "there is no Limit of Expansion; there is no Limit of Translucence / In the bosom of Man for ever from eternity to eternity." Los knows that we need only call on "ourselves, in whom God dwells," to find the "Divine Humanity" again. He seeks support from the cathedral cities in particular, asking that they counter the natural religion that builds Druid temples "instead of heavenly Chapels built / By our dear Lord."

Only Bath of the cathedral cities responds to Los's plea by saying that "none but the Lamb of God can heal / This dread disease, none but Jesus." Bath gets Oxford to "take . . . the leaves of the Tree of Life" (probably the Bible, printed in Oxford[4]), and Oxford asks Albion to stay with the cathedral cities until his perceptual and theological error can be removed: "Repose upon our bosoms / Till the plow of Jehovah and the Harrow of Shaddai / Have passed over the Dead to awake the Dead to judgment" (*CW,* 676). Albion, who has lost all other hope (*CW,* 677), submits and sinks into the arms of Jesus. He is put to sleep on a couch with 16 pillars that are made of the books of the Bible that Blake most admires.[5] Now Erin, the spirit of Ireland, is able to rise to speak about the errors of perception and thought that have led to Albion's plight:

> The Visions of Eternity, by reason of narrowed perceptions,
> Are become weak Visions of Time & Space, fix'd into furrows of
> death
>
> . . . .
>
> Withering the Human Form by Laws of Sacrifice for Sin. (*CW,* 679)

She announces the possibility of forgiveness of sins, for humans have done no more than fall into mistaken states of mind and perception. These mental states cannot be "forgiven," since they are errors, but individuals can be forgiven for their having entered such states. Therefore, she prays for the coming of Jesus with forgiveness of sins; and the Daughters of Beulah, carriers of artistic inspiration to a fallen world, respond: "Come then, O Lamb of God, and take away the remembrance of Sin" (*CW,* 681). And chapter 2 ends with Albion asleep on the bosom of the cathedral cities, and the coming of Jesus is awaited so that Albion can be restored.

Chapter 3

The third chapter of *Jerusalem* depicts the triumph of natural religion and natural morality and of the epistemology on which they are based. Accordingly, Blake's prefatory epistle, this time addressed "To the Deists," asserts that "he never can be a Friend to the Human Race who is the Preacher of Natural Morality or Natural Religion." Because Satan is the Accuser of Sin, "Every Religion that Preaches Vengeance for Sin is the Religion of the Enemy & Avenger and not of the Forgiver of Sin." Against the natural religionists, Blake identifies himself ("We") with "the Spiritually Religious," whether "a Monk, or a Methodist." He also defends Whitefield and, as would be expected, denounces Voltaire and Rousseau. Warfare is never caused by "poor Monks & Religious," he concludes, but by the natural religionists, a point that chapter 3 demonstrates.

In the lyric that follows and picks up these themes, Blake depicts a monk's suffering under a warlike state and moves to a defense of the emotions, "the little ones," that Albion rejected in chapter 2:

> Titus! Constantine! Charlemaine!
> O Voltaire! Rousseau! Gibbon! Vain
> Your Grecian Mocks & Roman Sword
> Against this image of his Lord!
>
> For a Tear is an Intellectual thing,
> And a Sigh is the Sword of an Angel King,
> And the bitter groan of a Martyr's woe
> Is an Arrow from the Almightie's Bow. (*CW,* 683)

"Fear and Hope are—Vision" (*CW,* 768), Blake wrote; and every Monk and Methodist knows that visionary truth resides in emotion, despite the natural religionists and despite Albion's present fallen condition.

Albion's rational power tells him that the "Friend of Sinners" is a "Rebel against my Laws"; he is ready to accept whatever the Daughters of Albion, the separated emanation of the Sons of Albion and the representatives of delusive nature, tell him. Los, however, labors on; he is building Golgonooza with the assistance of the Eternals, who always exist within the imagination to counteract the "generalizing Demonstrations of the Rational Power." The Daughters of Albion repeat Vala's assertion of the "female" power of nature over humanity:

> what may Woman be
> To have power over Man from Cradle to corruptible Grave?
> He who is an Infant and whose Cradle is a Manger
> Knoweth the Infant sorrow, whence it came and where it goeth
> And who weave it a Cradle of the grass that withereth away.
> This World is all a Cradle for the erred wandering Phantom,
> Rock'd by Year, Month, Day & Hour; and every two Moments
> Between dwells a Daughter of Beulah to feed the Human Vegetable.
> (*CW*, 688)

Only in the sustaining visits of inspiration by a Daughter of Beulah between "two moments" does humanity's real nutriment arrive. All that is subject to the Daughters of Albion, to "nature," is "the human Vegetable." But, arrogantly, the Daughters choose to misunderstand the Incarnation as proof that all is subject to nature.

Bath, Canterbury, York, and Edinburgh, the cathedral cities, join Los in his opposition to the Daughters of Albion to no avail. Jesus tries in vain to summon back Jerusalem, who is "clos'd in the Dungeons of Babylon," and only Los seems to hear Jesus say, "I am the Resurrection & the Life" and thus "live[s] and breathe[s] in hope"; for the intellectual side of humanity, represented by the Sons of Urizen, is now used to provide the technological means and ideological cover for human exploitation in alienated labor:

> Then left the Sons of Urizen the plow & harrow, the loom,
> The hammer & the chisel & the rule & compasses;
>
> . . . .
>
> And all the Arts of Life they chang'd into the Arts of Death in
> Albion.
> The hour-glass contemn'd because its simple workmanship
> Was like the workmanship of the plowman, & the water wheel

That raises water into cisterns, broken & burn'd with fire
Because its workmanship was like the workmanship of the shepherd;
And in their stead, intricate wheels invented, wheel without wheel,
To perplex youth in their outgoings & to bind to labours in Albion
Of day & night the myriads of eternity: that they may grind
And polish brass & iron hour after hour, laborious task,
Kept ignorant of its use: that they might spend the days of wisdom
In sorrowful drudgery to obtain a scanty pittance of bread,
In ignorance to view a small portion & think that All
And call it Demonstration, blind to all the simple rules of life. (*CW,*
699–700)

For most people, the division of labor has meant that the hope of doing work that is at the same time art has all but vanished. Instead the new industrial worker is permitted knowledge of only a narrow aspect of the production of the commodity. The "education" provided these workers gives them a faith in a rational Demonstration that offers "understanding" of the world but does not let them know that they can change it.

For the Sons of Albion, another result of such thought is war: not the intellectual wars of Eternity, but those carried out in behalf of jealousy and moral virtue—and in defense of the markets of the new exploitative industries—with the ordinary people of Britain again suffering most:

Is not the wound of the sword sweet & the broken bone delightful?
Wilt thou now smile among the scythes when the wounded groan in the field?
We were carried away in thousands from London & in tens
Of thousands from Westminster & Marybone, in ships clos'd up,
Chain'd hand & foot, compell'd to fight under the iron whips
Of our captains, fearing our officers more than the enemy. (*CW,* 700)

Through these acts, the sons of both Urizen and Albion contribute to the building of Stonehenge, the triumph of natural religion, where the sacrifice of children and the punishment of "sinners" can be carried out. One passage descriptive of Stonehenge summarizes much of Blake's thought about the triumph of natural religion:

The Building is Natural Religion & its Altars Natural Morality,
A building of eternal death, whose proportions are eternal despair,
Here Vala stood turning the iron Spindle of destruction
From heaven to earth, howling, invisible; but not invisible,
Her Two Covering Cherubs, afterwards named Voltaire & Rousseau,
Two frowning Rocks on each side of the Cove & Stone of Torture,
Frozen Sons of the feminine Tabernacle of Bacon, Newton & Locke;
For Luvah is France, the Victim of the Spectres of Albion. (*CW,* 702)

The worship of feminine "nature" has resulted from the empiricism of
"Bacon, Newton & Locke." Its result has been war on France that is to
Blake an effect of state religion, a secularized religion dominated by natural morality, that interests itself in statecraft to which it provides ideological resources.

Under the tyranny of natural religion, humanity's senses are made to
shrink, and the universe becomes even more alien:

The Stars flee remote; the heaven is iron, the earth is sulphur,
And all the mountains & hills shrink up like a withering gourd
As the Senses of Men shrink together under the Knife of flint
In the hands of Albion's Daughters among the Druid Temples.
(*CW,* 703)

Now the Daughters of Albion can be seen as Tirzah (the natural world)
and Rahab (corrupt, institutionalized religion). Together they preach
materialism: "Calling the Rocks Atomic Origins of Existence, denying
Eternity / By the Atheistical Epicurean Philosophy of Albion's Tree"
(*CW,* 704). They bring about the condemnation of Jerusalem, particularly the Liberty that she represents: "Drawing the free loves of Jerusalem
into infernal bondage / That they might be born in contentions of
Chastity & in Deadly Hate" (*CW,* 707).

The sex act is for most fallen humans their one imaginative act; therefore, since sex is their only insight into Jerusalem, this act must particularly be denounced by natural religion because it fears any outbreak of
the imaginative. Such an attitude, as we have seen before ("Brothels [are
built] with bricks of Religion"), creates "A Religion of Chastity, forming
a Commerce to sell Loves."

Hand has by now become a horrible analytic monster:

His bosom wide & shoulders huge, overspreading wondrous,
Bear Three strong sinewy Necks & Three awful & terrible Heads,
Three Brains, in contradictory council brooding incessantly,
Neither daring to put in act its councils, fearing each-other,
Therefore rejecting Ideas as nothing & holding all Wisdom
To consist in the agreements & disagreements of Ideas,
Plotting to devour Albion's Body of Humanity & Love. (*CW,* 708)

Within the monster, representing "Bacon & Newton & Locke" as well as
Hand, Rahab sits "Imputing Sin & Righteousness to Individuals" and
creating "Abstract Philosophy to destroy Imagination, the Divine
Humanity." And Rahab is in turn identified as Vala (*CW,* 709).

All the geography of the British Isles is, of course, a map of the fallen
Albion. In Eternity, all is human:

For all are Men in Eternity, Rivers, Mountains, Cities, Villages,
All are Human, & when you enter into their Bosoms you walk
In Heavens & Earths, as in your own Bosom you bear your Heaven
And Earth & all you behold; tho' it appears Without, it is Within,
In your Imagination, of Which this World of Mortality is but a
Shadow. (*CW,* 709)

And thus Blake devotes two plates (71 and 72) to outlining which parts
of England, Scotland, Wales, and Ireland belong to each of the Sons and
Daughters of Albion. Since Jerusalem will overspread all nations, he lists
the nations but combines them to reduce their number to 32. Missing
from these lists, however, is Golgonooza, which still belongs to Los.
Blake describes one of the gates of the New Jerusalem:

Fenelon, Guion, Teresa,
Whitefield & Hervey guard that Gate, with all the gentle Souls
Who guide the great Wine-press of Love. Four precious Stones that
Gate. (*CW,* 712)

Those who understand the role of emotion, who murder not "the little
ones," include the three great mystics (Fenelon, Guyon, Theresa of

Avila), the "Methodist" Whitefield, and the Evangelical Anglican Hervey; they have a special role to play in showing us the way back to the heavenly city.

Los struggles at his anvil to undo the works of Deists such as Voltaire, who would consider the limit of Opacity and the limit of Contraction not as the boundaries of our mental error but as proof of God's cruelty to mankind:

> Voltaire insinuates that these Limits are the cruel work of God,
> Mocking the Remover of Limits & the Resurrection of the Dead,
> Setting up Kings in wrath, in holiness of Natural Religion:
> Which Los with his mighty Hammer demolishes time on time
> In miracles & wonders in the Four-fold Desart of Albion. (*CW,* 713)

God removes limits and resurrects humanity; He does not impose limitation, and that this freedom is attainable the visionary artist can prove. Blake prays for the full inspiration that Los possesses:

> Teach me, O Holy Spirit, the Testimony of Jesus! let me
> Comprehend wonderous things out of the Divine Law!
> I behold Babylon in the opening Streets of London. I behold
> Jerusalem in ruins wandering about from house to house. (*CW,* 714)

He sees how bad theology and bad epistemology have brought bad art: "Harmonies of Concords & Discords / Opposed to Melody, and by Lights & Shades opposed to Outline, / And by Abstractions opposed to the Visions of Imagination" (*CW,* 715). He also sees how natural religion has brought sexual repression and war:

> Babylon, the Rational Morality, deluding to death the little ones
> In strong temptations of stolen beauty. I tell how Reuben slept
> On London Stone, & the Daughters of Albion ran around admiring
> His awful beauty; with Moral Virtue, the fair deciever, offspring
> Of Good & Evil, they divided him in love upon the Thames & sent
> Him over Europe, in streams of gore. (*CW,* 715)

Reuben, natural humanity and now the complete victim, passes into the bloody conflicts of Europe "in streams of gore."

All the centuries of false religion stand revealed to Blake from "Adam to Luther" and on through the natural religion of Rahab. But still Blake's vision can center on "Jesus, breaking thro' the Central Zones of Death & Hell, [who] / Opens Eternity in Time & Space, triumphant in Mercy" (*CW,* 716). Albion is fully fallen into the delusions of empiricism ("the starry Heavens are fled from the mighty limbs of Albion"), into the cruelties of natural morality, and into natural theology. But the prophets, Los and Blake, are ready to begin his restoration.

Chapter 4

The concluding chapter of *Jerusalem* is addressed to the Christians. The errors of the Deists have now solidified and become dominant in "Christian" England. Now, in Blake's own time, the Christians have reached a dead end that they can escape only by exercising the "Divine Arts of Imagination" rather than rationality and the systems of natural religion. Blake admits to the Satanic wheels that have come to dominate our perception:

> I stood among my valleys of the south
> And saw a flame of fire, even as a Wheel
> Of fire surrounding all the heavens: it went
> From west to east, against the current of
> Creation, and devour'd all things in its loud
> Fury & thundering course round heaven & earth.
> By it the Sun was roll'd into an orb,
> By it the Moon faded into a globe
> Travelling thro' the night. (*CW,* 717)

Such wheels are not only physical but also moral systems: "Is this the law of Jesus, / This terrible devouring sword turning every way?" Fortunately, the answer to Blake's question is no; what he sees is only the wheel of mistaken natural religion, while in truth "Jesus is the bright Preacher of Life / Creating Nature from this fiery Law / By self-denial & forgiveness of Sin" (*CW,* 718). "Creating Nature" in Blake's sense is uncreating the delusive nature that we see so that Eternity can be restored. This process of renewal is carried out not by application of the law but through "forgiveness," which destroys all systems of law. Blake ends his preface with another lyric that appeals for the restoration of Jerusalem to England.

Rahab, institutionalized natural religion, is seen as enthroned at the outset of chapter 4 with "power over the earth." Jerusalem is an outcast: "How distant far from Albion! his hills & valleys no more / Receive the feet of Jerusalem: they have cast me quite away, / And Albion is himself shrunk to a narrow rock in the midst of the sea!" (*CW,* 720). Vala in her confused state fears that, should Jesus return, He would revive Albion and permit him to slay her Luvah. Hand and Hyle are fully enslaved by their feminine emanations, Cambel and Gwendolen, who are separated objects of perception and who are therefore able to tyrannize over the perceiver as does the empiricist's world. Cambel and Gwendolen congratulate themselves on having driven away Merlin, the imaginative man; but they still fear that they will "perish annihilate" if they do not carry out their binding and limiting of the human mind with sufficient thoroughness.

Thus, on the surface, the situation seems little changed from chapter 3; but what is significantly different is the increasing note of desperation among the forces of evil. As Blake says, "he who will not bend to Love must be subdued by Fear." Natural religion proves inadequate to human needs, and rationality leads to the despair about reason's power and about human nature that the eighteenth century saw in David Hume. Error has taken definite shape, and it will make destruction all the easier to carry out.

Los is still dedicated to his vision, and has an ever-increasing sense of his powers and his role. The solidification of error and error's growing lack of confidence in itself will make his task easier to accomplish. Los can say, "I know I am Urthona, keeper of the Gates of Heaven / And that I can at will expatiate in the Gardens of bliss." He knows that Daughters of Albion, like those worshipped by Hand and Hyle, weave only "An outside shadowy Surface superadded to the real Surface / Which is unchangeable for ever & ever."

And Albion's daughters have a growing sense of loss, like that which characterized the work of Lord Byron, a knowledge of a lost paradise from which their rationality now bars them: "Our Father Albion's land, O it was a lovely land!" Once, as emanations of healthy Sons of Albion, "We builded Jerusalem as a City & a Temple; from Lambeth / We began our Foundations, lovely Lambeth" (*CW,* 729). They know that they are really enslaved now (even though they are in turn the enslavers of

Albion) because they are compelled to "build Babylon on Euphrates" in the service of mistaken notions of perception. They see what their labors have cost British civilization: "I see London, blind & age-bent, begging thro' the Streets / Of Babylon, led by a child" (*CW,* 729). They now fear even their victim Hand, who "combines into a Mighty-one, the Double Molech & Chemosh," the gods of sacrifice and war.

Los offers a Song in praise of his constant vision of Jerusalem within Albion:

I see thy Form, O lovely mild Jerusalem, wing'd with Six Wings
In the opacous Bosom of the Sleeper, lovely Three-fold
In Head & Heart & Reins, three Universes of love & beauty.
Thy forehead bright, Holiness to the Lord, with Gates of pearl
Reflects Eternity; beneath, thy azure wings of feathery down
Ribb'd delicate & cloth'd with feather'd gold & azure' & purple,
From thy white shoulders shadowing purity in holiness!
(*CW,* 730–31)

Los's artistic vision has achieved such clarity of outline that Eternity cannot be far off; but a last-ditch counterworld, based on a false definition of humanity, has also been under construction. The Daughters of Albion started it by building "a Space & an Allegory around the Winding Worm" that Hyle has become. This world is one that is institutionalized rather than spontaneous; it is "an Earthly Kingdom" where the Daughters of Albion "reign in pride & to oppress & to mix the Cup of Delusion." What they create is State Religion—religious insight that was forced into the framework of the state, as was to be found in Rome or that materialized in England under the Puritans. (The seeds of the spiritual kingdom must constantly be planted by the Daughters of Beulah, by inspiration.)

Los mistakenly brings Reuben (natural humanity) into this kingdom because of his artist's wish to make Enitharmon ("space") actually embody the ideal. But, since contact with institutions based on materialistic assumptions is always destructive of the spiritual, the result of this attempt is a repetition of the separation of Enitharmon from Los and finally the appearance of the Covering Cherub, the Anti-Christ of State Religion:

    in selfish holiness:
The Pharisaion, the Grammateis, the Presbuterion,
The Archiereus, the Iereus, the Saddusaion: double
Each withoutside of the other, covering eastern heaven.
Thus was the Covering Cherub reveal'd, majestic image
Of Selfhood, Body put off, the Antichrist accursed,
Cover'd with precious stones: a Human Dragon terrible
And bright stretch'd over Europe & Asia gorgeous.
In three nights he devour'd the rejected corse of death.
His Head, dark, deadly, in its Brain incloses a reflexion
Of Eden all perverted. (*CW,* 734)

Jerusalem is "Hidden within the Covering Cherub," and Los, whatever his mistakes before, knows that this institutionalized error must be
overcome:

Go to these fiends of Righteousness,
Tell them to obey their Humanities & not pretend Holiness
When they are murderers: as far as my Hammer & Anvil permit.
Go, tell them that the Worship of God is honouring his gifts
In other men: & loving the greatest men best, each according
To his Genius: which is the Holy Ghost in Man; there is no other
God than that God who is the intellectual fountain of Humanity.
He who envies or calumniates, which is murder & cruelty,
Murders the Holy-one. Go, tell them this, & overthrow their cup,
Their bread, their altartable, their incense & their oath,
Their marriage & their baptism, their burial & consecration.
I have tried to make friends by corporeal gifts but have only
Made enemies. I never made friends but by spiritual gifts,
By severe contentions of friendship & the burning fire of thought.
He who would see the Divinity must see him in his Children,
One first, in friendship & love, then a Divine Family, & in the midst
Jesus will appear; so he who wishes to see a Vision, a perfect Whole,
Must see it in its Minute Particulars, Organized, & not as thou,

O Fiend of Righteousness, pretendest; thine is a Disorganized
And snowy cloud, brooder of tempests & destructive War.
You smile with pomp & rigor, you talk of benevolence & virtue;
I act with benevolence & Virtue & get murder'd time after time.
You accumulate Particulars & murder by analyzing, that you
May take the aggregate, & you call the aggregate Moral Law,
And you call that swell'd & bloated Form a Minute Particular;
But General Forms have their vitality in Particulars, & every
Particular is a Man, a Divine Member of the Divine Jesus. (*CW,* 738)

The institution and rites of the church have been worshipped far more
than the God in every individual. Enitharmon—the projection of Los
just as the institutionalized church is the projection of the winding
worm—fears that she will "annihilate vanish for ever" (*CW,* 739). And,
in a sense, she must, because, as Los says, "Sexes must vanish & cease /
To be when Albion arises from his dread repose" (*CW,* 739). But the van-
ishing of sexes means simply that, in the case of Enitharmon, she will
return to the breast of Los, her source, even as "the Church," properly
understood, will return to the human heart.

Los now sees the coming of the Anti-Christ, the solidification of error,
as the promised signal for the apocalypse:

Fear not, my Sons, this waking Death; he is become One with me.
Behold him here! We shall not Die! we shall be united in Jesus.
Will you suffer this Satan, this Body of Doubt that Seems but Is
Not,
To occupy the very threshold of Eternal Life? if Bacon, Newton,
Locke
Deny a Conscience in Man & the Communion of Saints & Angels,
Contemning the Divine Vision & Fruition, Worshiping the Deus,
Of the Heathen, the God of This World, & the Goddess Nature,
Mystery, Babylon the Great, The Druid Dragon & hidden Harlot,
Is it not that Signal of the Morning which was told us in the
Beginning? (*CW,* 741)

And, indeed,

Time was Finished! The Breath Divine Breathed over Albion
Beneath the Furnaces & starry Wheels and in the Immortal Tomb,
And England, who is Brittannia, awoke from Death on Albion's
bosom:
She awoke pale & cold; she fainted seven times on the Body of
Albion.
"O pitious Sleep, O pitious Dream! O God, O God awake! I have
slain
In Dreams of Chastity & Moral Law: I have Murdered Albion! Ah!
In Stonehenge & on London Stone & in the Oak Groves of Malden
I have slain him in my Sleep with the Knife of the Druid. O
England!
O all ye Nations of the Earth, behold ye the jealous Wife!
The Eagle & the Wolf & Monkey & Owl & the King & Priest were
there." (*CW*, 742)

England returns to Albion's breast, putting an end to the concept of
a "state" that is external to us and makes laws for us: for Blake, as for
Marx, the state is needed only by those who use it to maintain oppression. Jesus appears:

    standing by Albion as the Good Shepherd
By the lost Sheep that he hath found, & Albion knew that it
Was the Lord, the Universal Humanity; & Albion saw his Form
A Man, & they conversed as Man with Man in Ages of Eternity.
And the Divine Appearance was the likeness & similitude of Los.
(*CW*, 743)

Jesus must resemble Los because both are the imagination. Jesus calls
Los to self-sacrifice, brotherhood, and the forgiveness of sins. Albion
picks up the "Bow of Mercy and Loving-kindness" and the "Arrows of
Love" and with them slays the "Druid spectre" of law and punishment.
"Milton & Shakspear & Chaucer," imaginative human beings, appear in
heaven as "Chariots of the Almighty"; but so do "Bacon & Newton &
Locke" because their previously one-sided systems now incorporate what
they before omitted.
    The human mind is free to create:

And they conversed together in Visionary forms dramatic which
bright
Redounded from their Tongues in thunderous majesty, in Visions
In new Expanses, creating exemplars of Memory and of Intellect,
Creating Space, Creating Time, according to the wonders Divine
Of Human Imagination. (*CW,* 746)

All false institutions and systems are gone (*CW,* 746); the world is at last
seen for what it is, a product of the imagination: "All Human Forms
identified, even Tree, Metal, Earth & Stone." All these are emanations
from us, existing only through the unifying activity of human perception
as do London, England, and the universe. In the aggregate, the projec-
tions from the divine imagination are Jerusalem: "And I heard the Name
of their Emanations: they are named Jerusalem" (*CW,* 747).

The Themes of *Jerusalem*

A specific concern that Blake pursues in *Jerusalem* is the restoration of the
English Church, which, he argues, must be freed from the secularization
seen in its involvement in political matters ("State Religion") and which
must be purged of its reliance on reason rather than on vision. Above all,
the Church must renounce the accusation of sin, Satan's province, and
adopt the forgiveness of sins to which Jesus summons it. In this respect,
Blake's themes in *Jerusalem* may seem "doctrinal," conditioned by his
wish to make "Lambeth" the center of a vital faith again. But we must
recognize that Blake's usual assumption that "all things Begin & End in
Albion's Ancient Druid Rocky Shore" is operative in *Jerusalem.* In seeking the restoration of a healthy theology to England, *Jerusalem* can picture the entire process by which the imagination is restored, despite the
threats and restrictions that it must overcome. Blake's last published
work, *Jerusalem* offers his message completely and triumphantly. Blake
never faltered in the faith that it sets forth.

Chapter Twelve

Conclusion

SUCH VISIONS HAVE APPEARED TO ME
AS I MY ORDERED RACE HAVE RUN.
JERUSALEM IS NAMED LIBERTY
AMONG THE SONS OF ALBION.
—*Jerusalem* (*CW,* 649)

The Themes of William Blake

William Blake's primary concern is the restoration to humankind of the clear vision and the perfect freedom of Eternity. He urges that all share in this "building up of Jerusalem," and he asks for the creation of an artistic and theological milieu in which "all the Lord's people" can be "Prophets." Some of his works describe how the fall from Eternity occurred and depict the destructive effects on the powers of the human mind that that fall has had. *The Book of Urizen* and *The Four Zoas* effectively recreate this process through their mythic presentation of the warring facilities—reason, imagination, energy, and integrative perception—faculties that must work in unison if we are to regain the genuine humanity of Eternity. In Eternity, Jesus—the Human Form Divine, ever present but denied by the rational faculty—will exist: "He in us, and we in Him." But, as *Milton* and *Jerusalem* make clear, a theology tied to nature and to moral codes, and one that does not practice the forgiveness of sins, cannot lead us back to our Divine Humanity. Such a theology does not free humanity but restricts it; it ignores the fact that Jerusalem is "named Liberty / among the sons of Albion."

Blake's definition of genuine liberty requires that we reject the illusion of humanity's having a place in the separated, crudely materialistic "nature" that the empiricist investigates. *The Book of Thel* and the three fine cyclical poems in the Pickering Manuscript show the limits of this falsely conceived world. We must learn to trust the intuition of the *Songs of Innocence* that humanity belongs to a better world than this one; we must see that the inadequate natural, social, and institutional world of

162

the *Songs of Experience* hovers on the brink of an apocalypse that threatens to erupt when we are bold enough to ask "The Tyger"—or any seemingly inhuman power in the world—why it exists. Blake's combined arts of poetry and engraving embody his views of nature. Every plate exists independently to offer within itself a specific statement on the inadequacy of the perspective depicted. The works are difficult for the "Corporeal Understanding," but they are meant to speak to the "Intellectual Powers." They deny, therefore, the validity of nature in the very mode by which they speak to us.

In works like *The Marriage of Heaven and Hell, Visions of the Daughters of Albion,* and *The French Revolution,* Blake attacks the codes of morality and the systems of law that deny the revolutionary energy in us that could lead us back to Eternity. He advocates "Impulse" and not "Rule," and he denies that we can make laws for others: "One Law for the Lion and the Ox is Oppression." Political revolutions, like those in France and America, reveal that the human mind is expanding toward the freedom of Eternity. Blake thus strongly advocates both sexual and political freedom, but he warns that they are productive of genuine liberty only when one's understanding of the relationship of subject and object and of the nature of human activity is built on better philosophic foundations than those of Paine or Voltaire, both of whom fell into the liberal trap of believing that radical political reform could occur in a world basically like the one envisioned by the ruling class of the time. Blake's determination to reconcile subject and object before setting out on the revolutionary path is shared by Karl Marx.

Blake as a Cultural Force

The scholarship of the last 70 years has made Blake sufficiently accessible to serious readers of poetry to allow him to challenge fundamental assumptions that are held by other authors in the literary canon and by the culture as a whole. Theodore Roszak (*The Making of a Counter Culture*) and Allen Ginsberg gave Blake a special role in their understanding of the "counter culture" that seemed to be emerging during the postwar economic boom that lasted until about 1974. In the 1970s, particularly, a wildfire spread of interest in Blake's work arose among students, and this engagement with him produced, if nothing else, a new generation of Blake scholars, each of whom has helped to spread aspects of Blake's counterhegemonic perspective even in conservative times. Blake remains in a position to become a significant force in revolutionizing the basis of our culture.

Blake's influence was felt from early in this century onwards in attempts to find a way out of what was once commonly called the "modern predicament"; Swinburne, Yeats, Lawrence, and Huxley are only a few of the modern authors who turned to Blake in their efforts to check the anguished drift toward nihilism that has characterized the modern temper. They saw, as we do, that Blake was a thinker who can show us how to transcend the habits of empiricism and rationality to which our minds have been bound since the work of Bacon, Newton, and Locke. At least three major Romantic poets in England offer to show us the way out: Blake, Wordsworth, and Coleridge. These writers all take as their subject the mind—its fall into error and its restoration to health through the imagination. But Blake perhaps succeeds best of these three by striking through the veil of error with the simple—not metaphorical but quite literal—statement that the imagination is Jesus. On the basis of this assertion, Blake's impressively coherent vision can offer a new morality and a new politics based on the eradication of all that restrains the imagination. Modernism was repeated as farce in what we now label Postmodernism, and the infection of the familiar intellectual triumvirate of Bacon-Newton-and-Locke continued to separate subject and object in such a way as to give us an alien universe in which action was impossible because of our uncertainty about the meaning of history. As the Modernist darkness has descended, language itself has come to be viewed as empty rhetoric rather than the tool for active intervention in the world that it is for William Blake—and for Karl Marx, who calls language "practical consciousness" (*M-E,* 158).

With Blake pointing to the way out of the Modernist dilemma, and having himself become the thinker with most influence in the twentieth century, there has indeed been Marx. Urging us not to stand back from the world in an effort to understand it, as the empiricist does, Marx invites us instead to change it, and this invitation cuts through the impasse of bourgeois philosophy as founded by Bacon-Newton-Locke (not to mention Hume and Kant); Marx's challenge restores to humanity both its engaged role in what is not an alien universe but a human one and allows humans to resume their defining life activity—which is, precisely, that of changing the world. If the socialist historian and theoretician E. P. Thompson had two sources of inspiration for his work ("my own pantheon"), Karl Marx and William Blake, he would have found little conflict between them. Blake and Marx emerge from the same philosophic outlook in their replies to the empiricists, and both confront Modernism by restoring to humanity a meaningful universe that responds to labor and to language. Blake and Marx share as well an understanding of the historic effects of the division of labor, an understanding of the character of both exploitation and oppression, and a commitment to revolution. In his own search for a way out of the long impasse of Modernism, Thompson seems right to have linked the two in proposing "the floor upon which the future must walk" (Thompson, 228).

One element in Blake that astonishes the modern reader and would make most Marxists uneasy is Blake's confident reliance on a Christian stance. Blake adheres to Christianity in the face of threats to it that neither twentieth-century science nor twentieth-century philosophy make more vigorously than they were made to Blake's age by David Hume. As eccentric a figure as Blake seemed to his readers in the first hundred years after his death, he now seems the one Romantic who most adheres to the defining force of Western civilization, Christianity. We can now understand Blake's easy linking of himself with Isaiah and Ezekiel and his contentions with fellow prophets such as Dante and Milton. We can now understand what he meant in saying that Wordsworth was not a "Bible Christian." Blake turns out after all to be the one Romantic who fits most comfortably into Judaeo-Christian traditions of thought and art. "Secular" approaches to Blake also had their successes, but Blake's theology is no longer ignored by serious Blakists. His special relevance to us all may well be in his offering to heal the crisis in our civilization by demonstrating that it is threatened with dissolution only because it fails to heed the Saviour, who is—literally for Blake—within each individual.

It is likely that no one would be more uncomfortable with Blake's Evangelical Christianity than Karl Marx himself. The specifics of Marx's objections to religion should, however, be looked at carefully: Marx explains that "for socialist man the *entire so-called history of the world* is nothing but the begetting of man through human labour," so "the question about an *alien* being above nature and man—a question which implies the admission of the inessentiality of nature and man—has become impossible in practice" (*M-E*, 92). Blake does *not*, however, conceive of God as an alien figure existing outside humanity—"All deities reside in the human breast"—or outside this world. Nor does Blake support any of the ideological uses to which the bourgeois state has put religion. In terms of the theistic thought that *both* Blake and Marx oppose, Marx's atheism is, as Denys Turner rightly says, "not anti- but postthe-

istic" and therefore "postatheistic" as well.[1] Marx himself declared that
"*atheism*" within a dialectical understanding of what is real "has no
longer any meaning" (*M-E,* 92), and Lenin saw philosophical idealism
and crude, metaphysical materialism as twin errors. Both Blake and
Marx have moved to the next stage of that dialectic, and Blake's work
could be read as setting forth the basis for a reconciliation of Christianity
and Marxism.

Critical theory has been caught up in the impasse of Modernism too,
and Marx and Blake offer similar guidance to those endeavoring to move
forward. Both Blake and Marx show us that the work of art is the product of human intervention in the world, breaking down the false
dichotomy of subject and object in carrying into practice the most
fundamental of human needs, the need to change the world. In this
enterprise, the literary artist uses the material human resource of language—which is practical consciousness. The resulting art object can be
"read" as one reads one of Blake's plates, as an index of the degree to
which individual and culture have moved toward rehumanization. Every
detail in the work can, if the critic is sufficiently perceptive, be described
in terms of whether it displays imagination that is free or fettered.
Northrop Frye, who named Blake as the major influence on his work,
initiated a criticism that spoke of the meaning of literary form in much
this way, but now the most Blakean criticism—criticism that shares
Blake's activist stance and linguistic confidence— seems to be written
by those who describe themselves as Marxists.

One such Marxist critic, Terry Eagleton, writes that although William
Blake, "writing before the emergence of historical materialism, cast his
critique of industrial capitalism in theological terms," no subsequent literary critique of capitalism "has ever exceeded its power."[2] To the English,
especially those in the labor movement or on the left, Blake is, for all his
difficulty, honored as a visionary voice speaking for the ordinary people
who have endured exploitation under the system that Blake was one of
the first to oppose. Plays, exhibits, and publications endlessly celebrate his
life and work. But even if Blake is one of those rare writers to whom
adhere the aspirations even of people whose interests are not primarily literary, he is also a major poet and a central one, and he is fully the product
of all that is vital in the history of Western thought and art.

Notes and References

For the convenience of the general reader, quotations from Blake's poetry and prose are based on *The Complete Writings of William Blake,* edited by Geoffrey Keynes (London: Oxford University Press, 1966), which was used for decades in Blake criticism and scholarship, including such reader's aids as S. Foster Damon's *A Blake Dictionary.* Over the last 30 years, many Blake scholars have come to feel that David Erdman's edition of *The Poetry and Prose of William Blake* (later retitled *The Complete Poetry and Prose of William Blake*) should be regarded as the standard text, but the Keynes edition remained an alternative "standard" edition. The best scholarly edition, and therefore the final court of appeal on most textual issues, is now, however, *William Blake's Writings,* edited in two volumes by G. E. Bentley, Jr. Since the general reader may find the Bentley edition too expensive and, because of the two-volume format, inconvenient, I refer to the Keynes edition here.

Page numbers in the Keynes edition are given after all set-off quotations from Blake (for example, *K,* 227) and after many of the quotations that are integrated into the body of the discussion. Occasionally, in the interests of a less cluttered presentation, page references are omitted after short quotations that seem easy to locate because of the context of the discussion. Quotation marks supplied by Keynes are omitted when my exposition has identified the speaker of the lines quoted not to be Blake himself.

Preface

1. Michael Ferber, *The Social Vision of William Blake* (Princeton: Princeton University Press, 1985), ix.

2. E. P. Thompson, *Witness against the Beast: William Blake and the Moral Law* (Cambridge: Cambridge University Press, 1993), 226; hereafter cited in the text. For my review of Thompson's book, see *Militant International Review* 58 (1994): 31–32.

3. Minna Doskow, "The Humanized Universe of Blake and Marx," in *Blake and the Moderns,* ed. Robert J. Bertholf and Annette S. Levitt (Albany: SUNY Press, 1982), 225–40; hereafter cited in text as Doskow 1982a.

4. David Erdman raised the possibility that Blake is perhaps to be considered an Anglican in "Blake's Early Swedenborgianism: A Twentieth-Century Legend," *Comparative Literature* 5 (1953): 247–57; cited hereafter in text and below as Erdman 1953. Erdman has not, however, pursued this possibility in his subsequent work on Blake.

5. Geoffrey Keynes, ed., *The Complete Writings of William Blake* (London: Oxford University Press, 1966), 689; hereafter cited in the text as *CW.*

6. John Brenkman, *Culture and Domination* (Ithaca: Cornell University Press, 1987), 137; hereafter cited in text.

7. Ernst Fischer is quoted in Paul Breines, "Marxism, Romanticism, and the Case of Georg Lukács: Notes on Some Recent Sources and Situations," *Studies in Romanticism* 16 (1977): 475. Breines's article (473–89) is itself an invaluable explanation both of the romantic element in the thought of Marx and of the restoration of Marx's romanticism to Marxist theory as carried out by Georg Lukács.

Chapter One

1. The most reliable of the nineteenth-century accounts of Blake's life is Alexander Gilchrist, *Life of William Blake, "Pictor Ignotus"* (London: Macmillan, 1863), 2 vols.; hereafter cited in text. Other nineteenth-century biographical accounts, all quite brief, are collected in G. E. Bentley, Jr., *Blake Records* (Oxford: Clarendon Press, 1970); hereafter cited in text and below as *BR*. Bentley presents a skillful compilation of all available facts about Blake and an intelligent evaluation of the work of the nineteenth-century biographers. In *Blake Records Supplement* (Oxford: Clarendon Press, 1988), cited hereafter in text and below as *BRS*, Bentley adds some newly discovered information.

2. For Law's influence on John Wesley, see Eric W. Baker, *A Herald of the Evangelical Revival* (London: Epworth Press, 1948).

3. For Law's impact on English Swedenborgians, see, for instance, Theodore Compton, *The Life and Correspondence of the Reverend John Clowes* (London: Longmans, Green and Company, 1874), 14–15; cited below as Compton.

4. T. B. Shepherd, *Methodism and the Literature of the Eighteenth Century* (London: Epworth Press, 1940), 243. Actually, Shepherd's comment is made in response to a similar remark by Gilbert Thomas.

5. W. E. Gladstone, *Correspondence on Church and Religion,* ed. D. C. Lathbury (London: John Murray, 1910), 1, 7–8.

6. See *BR,* 7–8.

7. See Nancy Bogen, "The Problem of Blake's Early Religion, *Personalist* 44 (1968): 509–22, and Erdman 1953.

8. This important new information was discovered by Charles Gardner, who made the involvement in parish life of the Blake family the foundation of his *Blake's Innocence and Experience Retraced* (London: Athlone Press, 1986); hereafter cited in text as Gardner 1986.

9. See *CW,* 868, and *BRS,* 7.

10. Blake's childhood visions were by no means unique in England in this period; for a similar event, see Compton, 37.

11. Stanley Gardner, *Blake* (London: Evans Brothers, 1968), 18–23; hereafter cited in text as Gardner 1968.

12. This account apparently has its origin in a letter written by Blake. See *BR,* 13 and note.

13. "One day . . . he declared that the Romish Church was the only one which taught the forgiveness of sins. . . . He had a sentimental liking for the Romish Church. . . " (Gilchrist, 1, 330).

14. James King, *William Blake: His Life* (London: Weidenfeld and Nicolson, 1991), 37.

15. The phrase appears in William Blake, *Selected Writings,* ed. Robert Gleckner (New York: Crofts Classics, 1967), xxiii, and in Kathleen Raine, *William Blake* (London: Thames and Hudson, 1970), 27.

16. Martin K. Nurmi, *William Blake* (London: Hutchinson, 1975), 35.

17. Samuel C. Chew, "The Nineteenth Century and After," in *A Literary History of England,* ed. Albert C. Baugh (New York: Appleton-Century-Crofts, 1948), 1130.

18. For Evangelicals at Percy Chapel, see David Dale Stewart, *Memoir of the Life of the Rev. James Haldane Stewart,* 2d ed. (London: Thomas Hatchard, 1857), esp. 61–170, and J. S. Reynolds, *The Evangelicals at Oxford, 1735–1871* (Abingdon, Oxford: Marcham Manor Press, 1975), 95.

19. Many critics find poems such as "Holy Thursday" in *Innocence* to be ironic in intention. This approach to the state of Innocence robs it of its visionary power. See chapter 7.

20. *BR,* 36. The words are taken from Bentley's summary of the resolutions passed at the meeting.

21. The signatures have not themselves survived but are transcribed in Swedenborgian records.

22. J. G. Davies, *The Theology of William Blake* (Oxford: Clarendon Press, 1948), 34.

23. Richard Price, "A Discourse on the Love of our Country," in *The Debate on the French Revolution, 1789–1800,* ed. Alfred Cobban (London: Nicholas Kaye, 1950), 63–64.

24. Hayley quoted in *BR,* 78. Hayley's correspondence in this period abounds in variations on this patronizing formula applied to Blake.

25. Frederick Tatham suggested that Blake's "eccentric speeches were thrown forth more as a piece of sarcasm upon the inquirer than from his real opinion." See Tatham, "Life of William Blake," *BR,* 529.

26. From a letter written by George Richmond and published in Gilchrist, 1:362.

27. From an anonymous account quoted—and defended—in *BR,* 373–74.

Chapter Two

1. For a condensed discussion of this process and its effect on the structure of the "narrative" portion of Blake's artistic product, see David V. Erdman, *The Poetry and Prose of William Blake* (Garden City, N.Y.: Doubleday, 1965), 712–13; hereafter cited in text and below as Erdman 1965.

2.   Karl Marx, "Economic and Philosophic Manuscripts of 1844,"
Marx-Engels Reader, 2d ed., ed. Robert C. Tucker (New York: W. W. Norton,
1978), 124, 77; subsequent quotations from Marx or Engels are based on this
collection, hereafter cited in the text as *M-E.*
3.   V. I. Lenin, *Collected Works* (London: Lawrence and Wishart, 1961),
38, 363; hereafter cited in text.
4.   Harold Bloom, "The Visionary Cinema of Romantic Poetry," in
William Blake: Essays for S. Foster Damon, ed. Alvin H. Rosenfeld (Providence:
Brown University Press, 1969), 22.
5.   See Karl Kroeber, "Graphic-Poetic Structuring in Blake's *Book of
Urizen,*" *Blake Studies* 3 (1970): 9: "The 'narrative flow,' so to speak, of the
prophecy is constrained . . . by the distinct aesthetic integrity of each engraved
plate." Cited below as Kroeber.
6.   Northrop Frye, "The Road of Excess," in *The Stubborn Structure:
Essays on Criticism and Society* (London: Methuen, 1970), 164, 162.
7.   S. Foster Damon, *William Blake: His Philosophy and Symbols* (Boston:
Houghton Mifflin, 1924), 354.
8.   Minna Doskow, *William Blake's "Jerusalem"* (Rutherford, N.J.:
Fairleigh Dickinson University Press, 1982), 15.
9.   Actually, "the plates cannot be shifted about absolutely arbitrarily"
(Kroeber, 13).
10.   S. Foster Damon, *A Blake Dictionary* (Providence: Brown University
Press, 1965), 419; cited below as Damon 1965.
11.   David Punter, *Blake, Hegel, and Dialectic* (Amsterdam: Rodopi,
1982), 108; hereafter cited in text.

Chapter Three

1.   Beilby Porteus, *Death: A Poetical Essay* (Philadelphia: William
Woodhouse, 1773), 20.

Chapter Four

1.   See "Blake and Swedenborg" in Davies, 31–53, for a good treatment of Blake's feelings about "this visionary."
2.   The Swedenborgian resolutions are quoted from Davies, 34.
3.   For an attempt to locate the issues at controversy, see John Howard,
"An Audience for *The Marriage of Heaven and Hell,*" *Blake Studies* 3 (1970): 19–52.
4.   Joseph Milner, quoted in Roland N. Stromberg, *Religious Liberalism
in Eighteenth-Century England* (London: Oxford University Press, 1954), 168.
5. Stromberg, 173.

Chapter Five

1.   The most complete and most influential attempt to explicate the
historical level of Blake's work is David V. Erdman, *Blake: Prophet Against
Empire,* 3d ed. (Princeton: Princeton University Press, 1977).

2.   See M. H. Abrams, "English Romanticism: The Spirit of the Age," in *Romanticism Reconsidered,* ed. Northrop Frye (New York: Columbia University Press, 1963), esp. 30–37.

3.   See Edmund Burke, "Reflections on the Revolution in France," in *Select Works,* ed. E. J. Payne (Oxford: Clarendon Press, n.d.), 2, 89: "But the age of chivalry is gone. . . . Never, never more, shall we behold that generous loyalty to rank and sex, that proud submission, that dignified obedience, that subordination of the heart, which kept alive, even in servitude itself, the spirit of an exalted freedom."

Chapter Seven

1.   Tom Dacre would have taken his name from having been a foundling at Lady Dacre's almshouses. See Gardner 1986, 67.

2.   For a full discussion of the critical controversy surrounding the meaning of "The Tyger," and for a different reading of the poem, see Morton D. Paley, "Tyger of Wrath," *PMLA* 81 (1966): 540–41.

3.   Soame Jenyns, *A Free Inquiry into the Nature and Origin of Evil* (London: R. and J. Dodsley, 1757), 179.

4.   See especially "The Everlasting Gospel" (*CW,* 750–53).

5.   *The Marriage of Heaven and Hell* (*CW,* 149).

6.   See William Law, *Selected Mystical Writings,* ed. Stephen Hobhouse (London: C. W. Daniel, 1938): "Thinking and willing are eternal, they never began to be. Nothing can think or will now, in which there was not will and thought from all Eternity" (p. 35); "And here you may behold the sure ground of the absolute impossibility of the annihilation of the soul" (p. 37).

7.   Sir Paul Harvey, *The Oxford Companion to English Literature,* rev. Dorothy Eagle, 4th ed. (Oxford: Clarendon Press, 1967), 94.

Chapter Eight

1.   Unfortunately, Erdman has in later editions attempted to merge the two versions, thereby ignoring his own sound arguments of 1965, including his appeal to the way that Blake had stitched the sheets together.

2.   Here, and throughout this book, I accept David Erdman's argument that Lambeth Palace "was in a sense the inner court of English Christianity. Indeed, Blake's tendency was to think of Lambeth as Christ's Bride, the Church." Erdman, "Lambeth and Bethlehem in Blake's Jerusalem," *Modern Philology* 48 (1951): 184–92; cited below as Erdman 1951.

Chapter Nine

1.   William Adams, "Aesthetics: Liberating the Senses," *The Cambridge Companion to Marx,* ed. Terrell Carver (Cambridge: Cambridge University Press, 1991), 252; this collection of essays is cited below as Carver.

Chapter Eleven

1. Cf. Harold Bloom, *Blake's Apocalypse* (Garden City, N.Y.: Doubleday, 1963), 368, on "this mild song."

2. See Damon 1965, 162–65, for a description, with an accompanying chart, of Golgonooza.

3. For Ephratah, see Damon 1965, 127. I equate Bethlehem ("City of the Woods in the Forest of Ephratah") and Lambeth, assuming that Blake considered Lambeth to mean "place of the Lamb," which was in fact an etymology put forward by a Dr. Ducarel in 1796. The subject is treated in Erdman 1951, 184–92, but Erdman does not equate Lambeth and Bethlehem.

4. The suggestion is made by William R. Hughes in his "simplified" edition of *Jerusalem* (London: George Allen and Unwin, 1964), 185: "The reference here is to Oxford as the nurse of poets and divines, and possibly also to the leaves of the Bible, the words of God which are printed there."

5. These are also the books of the Bible most admired by Swedenborg. See G. E. Bentley, Jr., "Blake and Swedenborg," *Notes and Queries,* n.s., 199, no. 1 (1954): 264–65, and Damon, *Blake Dictionary,* 45.

Chapter Twelve

1. Denys Turner, "Religion: Illusions and Liberation" in Carver, 337.

2. Terry Eagleton, *Walter Benjamin; or Towards a Revolutionary Criticism* (London: Verso, 1981), 177.

Selected Bibliography

There has been a vast outpouring of books that deal with Blake since 1977, so I have exercised considerable selectivity in preparing this updated version of what I continue to envision as a "sound and minimal" list for the student of Blake's work. I have felt obligated to list the books that influenced my own understanding of Blake, but I have also made an effort to include books that take a different approach to Blake than I do. Highly specialized books, sometimes ones that argue a narrow thesis, have been excluded. The bibliographies listed below can be consulted for additional titles.

Facsimiles of Blake's illuminated works, collections of his artwork, and accounts of Blake the painter are also generally excluded here as inappropriate to the bibliography of a book so exclusively concerned as this one is with Blake the poet; but two of the standard texts of the poetry and prose that are listed below now provide black-and-white reproductions of Blake's work in illuminated printing, and modern technology has made possible inexpensive color facsimiles.

PRIMARY SOURCES

Bentley, G. E., Jr., ed. *William Blake's Writings.* 2 vols. Oxford: Clarendon Press, 1978. These painstakingly prepared volumes, which reproduce or describe Blake's designs as well as providing a text, should now be considered the standard scholarly edition of Blake.

Erdman, David V., ed. *The Complete Poetry and Prose of William Blake.* Commentary by Harold Bloom. Rev. ed. Berkeley and Los Angeles: University of California Press, 1982. Now the text most often cited in Blake criticism, Erdman's editing is less conservative than Bentley's and restores deleted lines. Erdman does not, however, supply or regularize punctuation as do Keynes and—more cautiously than Keynes—Bentley.

————, ed. *The Illuminated Blake.* Garden City, N.Y.: Doubleday Anchor, 1974. Black-and-white reproductions of Blake's works in illuminated printing with somewhat speculative but interesting commentary.

Keynes, Geoffrey, ed. *The Complete Writings of William Blake.* London: Oxford University Press, 1966. In its various editions (from 1925 on) this text was used by all serious Blakists until the appearance of the first edition of Erdman's *Poetry and Prose* in 1965. Now an alternate "standard" edition.

————, ed. *The Letters of William Blake.* 3d ed. Oxford: Clarendon Press, 1980. The standard edition of the letters, although they appear in Bentley as well.

Ostriker, Alicia, ed. *William Blake: The Complete Poems.* Harmondsworth: Penguin Books, 1977. Ostriker accepts the text as established by Erdman in his first edition (incorporating, however, Night 7b into *The Four Zoas,* which Erdman had in 1965 considered to have been canceled in favor of Night 7a), and, like Erdman, she elects to spell and punctuate as Blake did, disagreeing at times with the way Erdman has read Blake's hand. Ostriker supplies extensive annotation, making this a fine classroom text.

Stevenson, W. H., ed. *Blake: The Complete Poems.* 2d ed. London: Longmans, 1989. Expertly annotated edition of the poetry, with modernized spelling and punctuation; excellent for classroom use.

SECONDARY SOURCES

Biographies

Bentley, G. E., Jr. *Blake Records.* Oxford: Clarendon Press, 1969. Expertly compiled, invaluable collection of the surviving documentary evidence about Blake.

———. *Blake Records Supplement.* Oxford: Clarendon Press, 1988. Documentary evidence about Blake not yet found when *Blake Records* was published in 1969. Bentley's introduction includes a brief biography of Blake based on the records.

Davis, Michael. *William Blake: A New Kind of Man.* Berkeley and Los Angeles: University of California Press, 1977. Davis uses *Blake Records* to update the earlier biographies.

Gilchrist, Alexander. *Life of William Blake.* London: Macmillan, 1863; reprint, London: Dent, 1945. Most reliable of the few attempts that have been made to write a biography of Blake. Students should now supplement with the materials available in *Blake Records* and *Blake Records Supplement.*

King, James. *William Blake: His Life.* London: Weidenfeld and Nicolson, 1991. Using *Blake Records* to update Gilchrist and Wilson, King provides a readable new biography of Blake.

Lindsay, Jack. *William Blake: His Life and Work.* London: Constable, 1978. Probably the best biography of Blake published since Gilchrist, Lindsay's book offers little not available elsewhere but makes good use of Bentley's *Blake Records* and the other sources. Lindsay, an Australian who became one of England's most productive Marxist intellectuals, published his first book on Blake in 1927 and considered Blake a major influence on his own thought: Lindsay sees Blake's "ultimate kinship with the Marx of the 1844 Manuscripts."

Lister, Raymond. *William Blake: An Introduction to the Man and to His Work.* Foreword by G. E. Bentley, Jr. London: G. Bell and Sons, 1968. Enthusiastic biography by a man well qualified in the fine arts.

Wilson, Mona. *The Life of William Blake*. Edited by Geoffrey Keynes. London: Oxford University Press, 1971. Updating by Keynes of a sympathetic and generally accurate account of Blake the man. Suffers somewhat, however, from a forcing of the life into the patterns of "the Mystic Way." Previous editions in 1927 and 1948.

Wittreich, Joseph Anthony, Jr., ed. *Nineteenth-Century Accounts of William Blake*. Gainesville, Fla.: Scholars' Facsimiles, 1970. Convenient collection of a few other attempts at writing the Blake biography, but superseded by *Blake Records*.

Criticism

Adams, Hazard. *William Blake: A Reading of the Shorter Poems*. Seattle: University of Washington Press, 1963. Important attempt to read Blake's lyrics from the perspective provided by reading his longer and more difficult works.

Altizer, Thomas J. J. *The New Apocalypse: The Radical Christian Vision of William Blake*. East Lansing: Michigan State University Press, 1967. Study of Blake carried out by a major twentieth-century theologian.

Ault, Donald D. *Visionary Physics: Blake's Response to Newton*. Chicago: University of Chicago Press, 1974. Demonstrates way in which Blake interpreted Newtonian concepts and transformed them into poetic images.

Beer, John. *Blake's Humanism*. Manchester: Manchester University Press, 1968. *Blake's Visionary Universe*. Manchester: Manchester University Press, 1969. Ambitious and generally successful attempt to describe Blake's thought and art.

Blackstone, Bernard. *English Blake*. Cambridge: Cambridge University Press, 1949. Sound study of many aspects of Blake's thought, especially in its relationship to Bacon, Newton, Locke, and Berkeley. Like many other excellent Blakists of an earlier generation, however, Blackstone tends to ignore the extent to which Blake's Christianity is both literal and traditional.

Bloom, Harold. *Blake's Apocalypse*. Garden City, N.Y.: Doubleday, 1963. Brilliant critic's poem-by-poem presentation of Blake, with special emphasis on Blake's achievement as an epic poet.

Brenkman, John. *Culture and Domination*. Ithaca: Cornell University Press, 1987. This study of cultural practices in terms of the relationships of domination contains a good chapter on Blake that includes comparisons with Marx.

Bronowski, Jacob. *William Blake and the Age of Revolution*. New York: Harper and Row, 1965. Attractive account of Blake's life and times, but marred by an overinsistence on Blake as anti-industrialist. The book is a "new edition" of Bronowski's *William Blake: A Man without a Mask* (London: Seeker and Warburg, 1944), but actually adds only a new introduction.

Crehan, Stewart. *Blake in Context.* Dublin: Gill and Macmillan, 1984. This
      Marxist study identifies Blake's "particular moment in the class struggle"
      by emphasizing the political and religious concerns of Blake's London
      environment.
Curran, Stuart, and Joseph Anthony Wittreich, Jr., eds. *Blake's Sublime Allegory:
      Essays on "The Four Zoas," "Milton," and "Jerusalem."* Madison: University
      of Wisconsin Press, 1973. Essays evaluate both the visual and the poetic
      aspects of Blake's achievement.
Damon, S. Foster. *William Blake: His Philosophy and Symbols.* Boston: Houghton
      Mifflin, 1924. Pioneering work in Blake criticism. The information on
      Blake's sources and on the symbolic meaning of his mythic figures pro-
      vides the foundation for all subsequent readings of Blake, even though
      Damon's judgments are often highly intuitive.
Damrosch, Leopold, Jr. *Symbol and Truth in Blake's Myth.* Princeton: Princeton
      University Press, 1980. Damrosch studies unresolved contradictions in
      Blake's thinking.
Davies, J. G. *The Theology of William Blake.* Oxford: Clarendon Press, 1948.
      Careful, usually accurate report on Blake's religious opinions; has not
      received sufficient attention from Blake scholars.
DiSalvo, Jackie. *War of Titans: Blake's Critique of Milton and the Politics of Religion.*
      Pittsburgh: University of Pittsburgh Press, 1984. In this stimulating
      Marxist study, DiSalvo reads Blake's *Four Zoas* as a historical epic that
      traces human development from the time of primitive communism to the
      egalitarian society of the future; Blake challenges the myths of social and
      cultural evolution that were promulgated by bourgeois culture and
      endorsed by John Milton.
Dorfman, Deborah. *Blake in the Nineteenth Century: His Reputation as a Poet from
      Gilchrist to Yeats.* New Haven: Yale University Press, 1969. There were a
      few significant exceptions to the neglect Blake's work suffered until very
      recent times, and Dorfman usefully documents them in this study.
Doskow, Minna. "The Humanized Universe of Blake and Marx." In *William
      Blake and the Moderns,* edited by Robert J. Bertholf and Annette S. Levitt,
      225–40. Albany: State University of New York Press, 1982. This bril-
      liant essay provides the necessary foundation for a Marxist reading of
      Blake by demonstrating that Blake and Marx had a similar philosophic
      outlook, particularly in their explication of the relationship between sub-
      ject and object and in their assertion of the centrality of the labor process.
Eaves, Morris. *William Blake's Theory of Art.* Princeton: Princeton University
      Press, 1982. Eaves uses Blake's own statements to explain Blake's philos-
      ophy of art.
Erdman, David V. *Blake: Prophet against Empire.* 3d ed. Princeton: Princeton
      University Press, 1977. A triumph of research, this book demonstrates
      Blake's extensive use of the events and moods of his own age.

Increasingly, critics have questioned whether Blake incorporated quite as much of contemporary politics as Erdman suggests, and Erdman has himself reconsidered many points in his two revisions of the book.

————, and John E. Grant, eds. *Blake's Visionary Forms Dramatic.* Princeton: Princeton University Press, 1969. Collection of essays that focus on the pictorial side of Blake's creativity. Taken together, these essays form the best treatment of this aspect of Blake's achievement.

Essick, Robert. *William Blake and the Language of Adam.* Oxford: Clarendon Press, 1989. An approach to Blake through linguistic theory.

Ferber, Michael. *The Social Vision of William Blake.* Princeton: Princeton University Press, 1985. Excellent study of Blake's participation in, and continuing relevance for, the struggle for liberation and social justice.

Fisher, Peter F. *The Valley of Vision.* Edited by Northrop Frye. Toronto: University of Toronto Press, 1961. Major study of Blake's thought from a history of ideas perspective.

Frosch, Thomas R. *The Awakening of Albion: The Renovation of the Body in the Poetry of William Blake.* Ithaca: Cornell University Press, 1974. Exploration of "Albion's resumption of consciousness and of Blake's participation in the Romantic spirit of a complete human renewal, a spirit fundamentally secular."

Frye, Northrop. *Fearful Symmetry: A Study of William Blake.* Princeton: Princeton University Press, 1947. First book to offer a fully coherent picture of Blake's overall philosophy and aesthetic. The best book on Blake.

————. "The Keys to the Gates." In *Some British Romantics,* edited by James V. Logan, John E. Jordan, and Northrop Frye, 3–40. Columbus: Ohio State University Press, 1966. Outstanding but quite brief account of Blake's system.

Gardner, Stanley. *Blake.* London: Evans Brothers, 1968. Remarkable for the achievement of a good sense of Blake's presence as a Londoner. Omits consideration of Blake's epics; offers some good independent readings of the shorter poems.

————. *Blake's Innocence and Experience Retraced.* London: Athlone Press, 1986. An extremely important book that uses new evidence of the Blake family's ties to the Parish of St. James, Piccadilly, to argue that the *Songs of Innocence* celebrate the achievements of the local Church of England charity school and its country offshoot in Wimbledon.

Gleckner, Robert. *The Piper and the Bard.* Detroit: Wayne State University Press, 1959. Good study of the lyrics and of the concepts of Innocence and Experience.

Glen, Heather. *Vision and Disenchantment: Blake's "Songs" and Wordsworth's "Lyrical Ballads."* Cambridge: Cambridge University Press, 1983. Marxist in outlook, this book finds questioning of ruling-class ideology in both *Innocence* and *Experience.*

Hagstrum, Jean H. *William Blake: Poet and Painter*. Chicago: University of
    Chicago Press, 1964. Pioneering attempt to interpret the "composite art"
    of Blake's illuminated works.
Harper, George Mills. *The Neoplatonism of William Blake*. Chapel Hill: University
    of North Carolina Press, 1961. Interesting argument for the possible
    influence on Blake of Thomas Taylor, a contemporary Neoplatonic
    thinker. Kathleen Raine is one major Blakist sympathetic to Harper's
    position; otherwise, few find it useful to study Blake in these terms.
Hilton, Nelson. *Literal Imagination*. Berkeley and Los Angeles: University of
    California Press, 1983. Hilton studies Blake's words and images rather
    than larger structures such as myth.
Hirsch, E. D., Jr. *Innocence and Experience: An Introduction to Blake*. New Haven:
    Yale University Press, 1964. Attempt to demonstrate the development of
    Blake's thought and to deny that Blake's work has the monolithic coher-
    ence seen by Frye and most other critics. This argument has generally
    been ignored.
Hirst, Désirée. *Hidden Riches: Traditional Symbolism from the Renaissance to Blake*.
    New York: Barnes and Noble, 1964. Hirst studies the transmission from
    the Renaissance (through Boehme, William Law, Swedenborg, and eigh-
    teenth century religious groups) of Neoplatonism and Hebrew mysticism
    and shows how such elements are reflected in Blake's work.
Kroeber, Karl. "Graphic-Poetic Structuring in Blake's *Book of Urizen*." *Blake
    Studies* 3 (Fall 1970): 7–18. Best brief account of the aesthetic issues
    raised in Blake's unique artistic production, the illuminated "narrative."
    Good supplement to the material in the Erdman and Grant collection
    and in the Hagstrum book.
Larrissy, Edward. *William Blake*. Preface by Terry Eagleton. Oxford: Basil
    Blackwell, 1985. Larrissy shows that Blake's thoroughgoing political rad-
    icalism causes him to extend his critique to his own artistic method so
    that the reader must continually question and struggle to interpret.
Leader, Zachary. *Reading Blake's Songs*. London: Routledge and Kegan Paul,
    1981. Leader discusses the *Songs* in terms of children's books and educa-
    tional works of the period and "reads" the designs as well as the poems.
Lowery, Margaret R. *Windows of the Morning: A Critical Study of William Blake's
    "Poetical Sketches."* New Haven: Yale University Press, 1940. Useful study
    of Blake's emergence from his eighteenth-century poetic milieu.
McCalman, Iain. *Radical Underworld: Prophets, Revolutionaries and Pornographers in
    London, 1795–1840*. Cambridge: Cambridge University Press, 1988.
    Although not about Blake, this book offers a necessary portrait of Blake's
    political milieu through an account of radical figures who often shared
    Blake's language and aspects of his outlook.
Mee, John. *Dangerous Enthusiasm: William Blake and the Culture of Radicalism
    in the 1790s*. Oxford: Clarendon Press, 1992. Mee places Blake within
    the radical politics of his time, not through Blake's references to spe-

cific events and issues but through his use of the radical rhetorical practices of enthusiastic Christianity, literary primitivism, and biblical studies.

Mellor, Anne Kostelanetz. *Blake's Human Form Divine*. Berkeley: University of California, 1974. Study of Blake's "visual verbal art" finds "conflict between his philosophical theory and artistic practice, between his philosophical rejection of the human body and his aesthetic glorification of the human figure."

Mitchell, W. J. T. *Blake's Composite Art: A Study of the Illuminated Poetry*. Princeton: Princeton University Press, 1978. Mitchell studies the dialectical relationship between Blake's texts and designs.

Morton, A. L. *The Everlasting Gospel*. London: Lawrence and Wishart, 1958. Reprinted in A. L. Morton, *The Matter of Britain*, 88–121. London: Lawrence and Wishart, 1966. Reprinted again in *History and the Imagination: Selected Writings of A. L. Morton*, edited by Margot Heinemann and Willie Thompson, 106–46. London: Lawrence and Wishart, 1990. This brief, influential study demonstrates that the radical religious groups of the seventeenth century (such as the Ranters) anticipated (and probably influenced) Blake's rejection of the Moral Law, his advocacy of the equality of all people, and his denunciations of the powerful, and it shows how these groups expressed themselves in language much like Blake's.

Murry, J. Middleton. *William Blake*. London: Jonathan Cape, 1933. Murry understands and explicates Blake's fusion of visionary Christianity and radical politics well, and this book remains a valuable introduction to Blake more than 60 years after its publication.

Nurmi, Martin K. *William Blake*. London: Hutchinson, 1975. Impressive brief study.

Paley, Morton D. *The Continuing City: William Blake's "Jerusalem."* Oxford: Clarendon Press, 1983. The most complete guidebook to Blake's masterwork.

———. *Energy and the Imagination*. Oxford: Clarendon Press, 1970. Intelligent, well-informed study of what are perhaps the two crucial concepts in Blake's thought.

———, and Michael Phillips, eds. *William Blake: Essays in Honour of Sir Geoffrey Keynes*. Oxford: Clarendon Press, 1973. "The essays in this volume range in subject-matter from the earliest of Blake's writings and art to the works and friendships of his last years and the vicissitudes of his posthumous reputation."

Punter, David. *Blake, Hegel, and Dialectic*. Amsterdam: Rodopi, 1982. This important book places Blake along with Hegel (and Marx) within a revival of the dialectical method of thought first seen in Heraclitus: as a dialectical thinker Blake can avoid the subjectivism and metaphysics of other Romantics.

Raine, Kathleen. *Blake and Tradition.* 2 vols. Princeton: Princeton University Press for the Bollingen Foundation, 1968. The product of a lifelong study of Blake and of the "heterodox tradition" in religion and philosophy, these handsome volumes set forth significant analogues and sources for Blake's art and ideas. As with Damon, another specialist in the heterodox, a few of the conclusions seem overly intuitive.

Rosenfeld, Alvin H., ed. *William Blake: Essays for S. Foster Damon.* Providence: Brown University Press, 1969. Handsome tribute to a widely influential Blakist and a fascinating sampling of the interests of some outstanding scholars who continued Damon's work.

Rothenberg, Mary Ann. *Rethinking Blake's Textuality.* Columbia: University of Missouri Press, 1993. Rothenberg argues that, because Blake recognized the epistemological crisis that would characterize modernity, he could offer insights that anticipated the poststructuralists.

Schorer, Mark. *William Blake: The Politics of Vision.* New York: Holt, 1946. Although the book is especially good on the political contexts of Blake's thought, it also serves the general reader as a sound introduction to most of Blake's related concerns.

Singer, June K. *The Unholy Bible: A Psychological Interpretation of William Blake.* New York: G. P. Putnam's Sons for the C. G. Jung Foundation, 1970. A Jungian study of Blake is a good idea, but this book accepts too many of the biographical legends about Blake to be at all convincing to the Blake scholar.

Tannenbaum, Leslie. *Biblical Tradition in Blake's Early Prophecies: The Great Code of Art.* Princeton: Princeton University Press, 1982. Tannenbaum studies Blake's use of the Bible and its commentators.

Thompson, E. P. *Witness against the Beast: William Blake and the Moral Law.* Cambridge: Cambridge University Press, 1993. New York: New Press, 1993. This book marks an important return to an emphasis on the similarities between Blake's ideas and language and the writings of the radical religious groups of the seventeenth century (see Morton), but Thompson especially emphasizes the Muggletonians, a sect that existed until recent years. A disappointing feature is that Thompson, a distinguished socialist historian and theoretician, does not develop comparisons between Blake and Marx as thinkers.

Wagenknecht, David. *Blake's Night: William Blake and the Idea of Pastoral.* Cambridge: Harvard University Press, 1973. Studies Blake's poetry "in terms of a single, unifying thematic concern or idea: the idea of pastoral."

Wittreich, Joseph Anthony, Jr. *Angel of Apocalypse: Blake's Idea of Milton.* Madison: University of Wisconsin Press, 1975. "As a critic of Milton, Blake is peerless: his understanding far outruns the understanding of Milton that dominated the nineteenth century."

Youngquist, Paul. *Madness and Blake's Myth*. University Park: Pennsylvania State University, 1989. Youngquist argues that Blake's myth dramatizes Blake's own psychological conflicts.

Bibliographies

Bentley, G. E., Jr. *Blake Books*. Oxford: Clarendon Press, 1977. A revised edition of G. E. Bentley, Jr., and Martin K. Nurmi, *A Blake Bibliography* (Minneapolis: University of Minnesota Press, 1964), this indispensable volume lists Blake's writings in illuminated printing and conventional printing and in manuscripts, catalogs his designs and his engravings for books, surveys books that Blake is known to have owned, and records and annotates writing about Blake published before June 1974.

Johnson, Mary Lynn. "William Blake." In *The English Romantic Poets*, edited by Frank Jordan, 113–253. New York: Modern Language Association, 1985. Carefully considered, detailed survey of Blake scholarship.

Natoli, Joseph P. *Twentieth-Century Blake Criticism: Northrop Frye to the Present*. New York: Garland, 1982. Annotated bibliography of Blake criticism published between 1947 and 1982, arranged under categories such as "Blake's Symbols and Themes," "Blake's Influence," "Sources and Analogues," and "Critical Comparisons."

Reference

Damon, S. Foster. *A Blake Dictionary*. Providence: Brown University Press, 1965. A study of Blake's philosophy and symbols presented in "dictionary" format by the father of American Blake studies.

Erdman, David V. *A Concordance to the Writings of William Blake*. Ithaca: Cornell University Press, 1967. 2 vols.

Index

The Author

Victor N. Paananen is Professor of English at Michigan State University. He received the bachelor of arts degree from Harvard University magna cum laude and was elected to Phi Beta Kappa. He subsequently earned the master of arts and doctor of philosophy degrees from the University of Wisconsin at Madison, where he held the University Fellowship. Dr. Paananen has been at Michigan State since 1968 and has served there as assistant dean of the graduate school (1977–82) and chairperson of the Department of English (1986–94). He has also taught at Wofford College (1962–63), at Williams College (1966–68), and, as a visiting professor, at Roehampton Institute in London (1982). In 1992, he was made an honorary fellow of Roehampton Institute. He is the author of *William Blake* (1977) in Twayne's English Authors Series, has published articles on Lord Byron, on the Anglican Evangelical Martin Madan, on religious doubt in British literature, and on Dylan Thomas, and has contributed 10 articles on British literary and political figures to the *Biographical Dictionary of Modern British Radicals*.